Heidelberg

Holly Myers

then/and

© Holly Myers, 2021.
then/and publications
ISBN: 978-1-947322-01-1

Storyline   5

Mapwalkers   49

Heidelberg   95

Storyline

A man in the early days of his career is hired as second in command of an aged ship with a religious name on a journey from one side of the world to another. The ship is to carry a load of coal. Within a week of its departure, the ship is battered in a storm and towed into a port not far from the first, where it remains docked for a month. The night before it is to leave again, its fore-rigging is smashed by a passing ship and its departure is delayed another three weeks. When it leaves at last, it meets with fine weather at first, then terrible wind for days on end. The ship begins to leak and the pumps malfunction; the crew members must pump out the water themselves. Parts of the ship begin to fall off. The sails blow away. The kitchen blows off and the cook goes mad. Eventually, the wind dies down and the ship makes it back to shore, at another port still in the country of its origin. It remains there for six months, a laughingstock, departing several times only to fill with water and return again, until the ship's owner at last approves a comprehensive repair. The ship leaves again and this time makes it most of the way to its destination; then the coal in the hull of the ship combusts. For some time, the crew fights off a fire it cannot see, only smell. The men first attempt to smother the fire, then flood it. It appears for a time to have gone out. The crew congratulates itself. Then an explosion blows up the deck. No one is killed but everyone is injured. A passing ship that is carrying mail agrees to tow the ship to the nearest port; however, the speed of the journey fans the flames in the hull and soon the ship begins to really burn. The captain insists on remaining with the ship so as to salvage what he can on behalf of its investors and the ship carrying the mail goes on. The crew enjoy one last crazed meal aboard the burning ship. The captain falls asleep on a cushion. Then the crew departs in three boats as the aged ship with the religious name goes down. The man in his youth reaches the other side of the world at last at the helm of the smallest of the three boats.

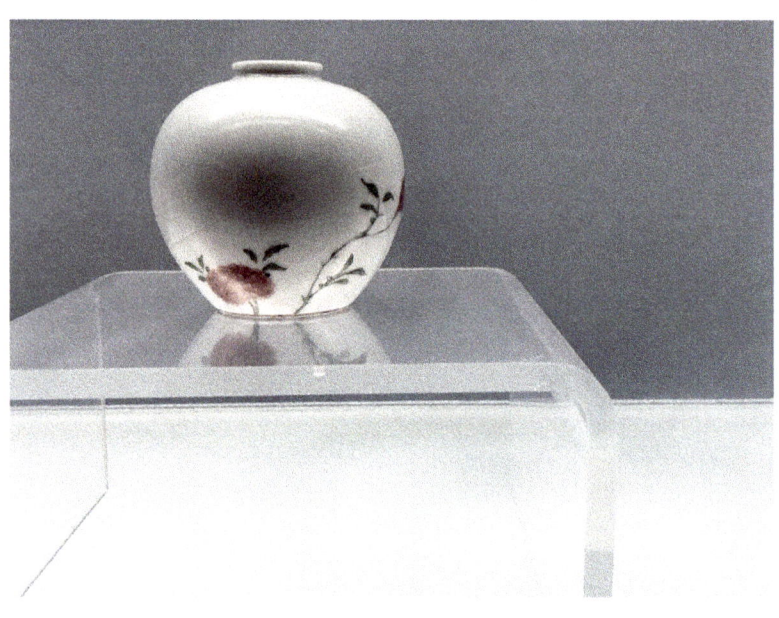

A man makes a deal with one enemy to protect his wife, whom he loves, from the threat of another enemy. The first is an abstract and impersonal enemy: an enemy of the state, not of himself. The second is a personal one, proximate and dangerous, capable of inflicting upon both him and his wife humiliation, imprisonment, bodily violence and death. The man succeeds in removing to safety, to the country where he's from—a country very far from the country where they are—both his wife and her child, whom he adopts as his own, and they live together in a state of great personal happiness for seven years. However, the deal is an ongoing deal, requiring continued periodic actions on his part and thus continued vigilance and secrecy, even from his wife. The secrecy wears on him. One day, an innocent man is killed as a result of the deal he made with the abstract enemy. Around the same time, his own people—that is, those who share his nationality and by whom he is actually employed—enter into a deal of their own, forming an alliance with the personal enemy against the abstract one, which both consider to be a threat. Here, the man has a choice to make. If he accepts the death of the innocent man as signaling the end of the deal, as the abstract enemy is prepared by necessity to do, he would be cleared. The dead man would take the blame and he would be free to live in peace with his wife and their child. If he retaliates against his own people, whether out of guilt for causing the innocent man's death or resistance against the deal his own people have forged with his personal enemy, he will be exposed, and the great personal happiness in which he has lived hitherto in relative safety for seven years and for which he has sacrificed so much to this point will be destroyed. He chooses the latter, using the power he has by way of this deal against his own people in favor of the abstract enemy, then retreats in the only direction he can: that is, into the protection of the abstract enemy, in a country very far from his own. To do so, he must leave his wife in the protection of his own people, who are not her people, in the belief that she will join him soon. His own people cannot, in fact, stop her from joining him, but they can stop her son, a minor, and they do. Thus, she is faced with a choice of her own: her husband or her son, and she chooses her son. She must. His own people, then, become a new kind of enemy, his own country a new kind of prison for his wife, while he is branded by even his own mother a traitor.

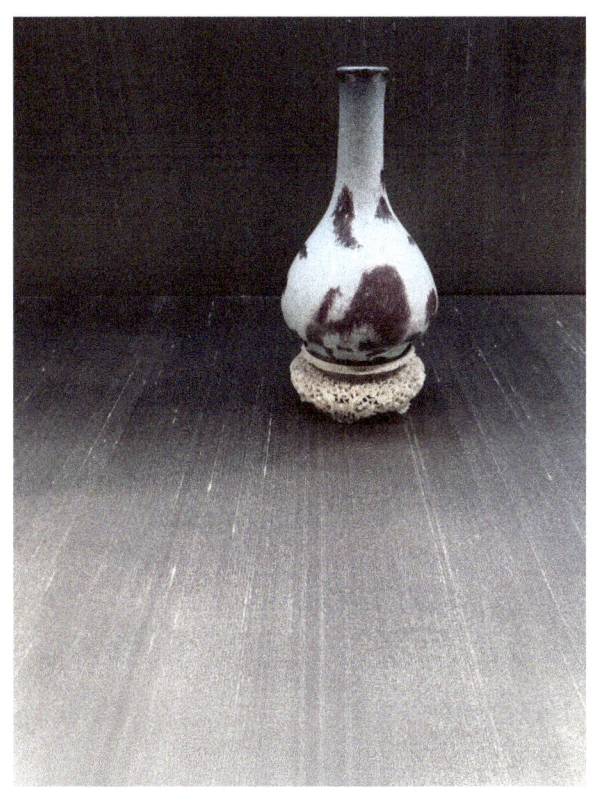

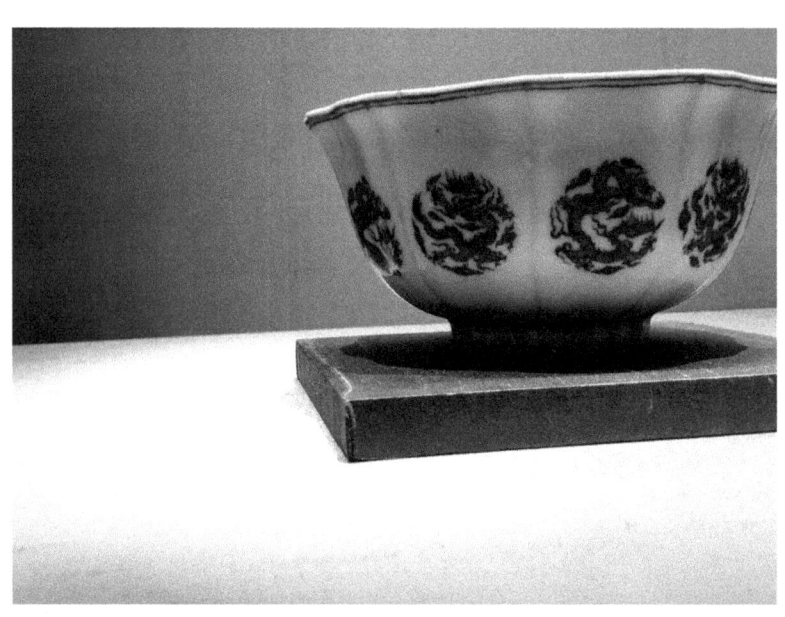

A man who was raised by a pessimistic widower who breeds in him a harsh philosophical instinct lives an itinerate, solitary life in a country very far from the country of his birth. He meets a ship captain who's hard on his luck and offers the captain a small loan, saving him from ruin. Then the captain builds a coal mine on an island and hires the man to oversee it. Shortly thereafter, the captain dies and the mine goes bankrupt, though the man chooses to remain on the island, alone with a single servant of a different race. While visiting a nearby island for provisions, the man meets a girl who plays in a hotel band. She, too, is in trouble; she is alone in the world, and neither the hotel proprietor, who desires her, nor the proprietor's wife, who resents her, will leave her be. The man takes the girl with him back to his island, where they live in a quiet state of mutual respect and love. Then a mysterious trio of unsavory characters appears at the hotel. The proprietor, filled with rage at his loss of the girl and also wanting to be rid of the unsavory characters, tells them, falsely, that the man is hiding treasure on his island and tells them how to get there. The unsavory characters go to the island, aiming to kill the man and claim the treasure. One of the three tries to kill the girl, then falls in love with her. She plays along at first, but when he is kissing her foot, she kicks him in the neck. The second character, who despises all women, then kills the girl with a shot intended for the first character. The first character flees and the second disappears. The captain of a passing ship, alerted by the wife of the hotel proprietor, lands on the island in time to watch the girl die. The second character shoots the first one again, hitting him in the heart this time, and the first character dies. The third character, who has remained in the boat, is shot by the servant of another race, who then pushes the boat out to sea. The second character drowns, possibly trying to reach the boat, possibly by suicide, knowing he is doomed. The man sets his house ablaze with the girl and himself inside. He dies. The passing ship captain reports the whole sad story to a public official. The servant of another race travels to the other side of the island to retrieve his wife, who's been living in a village there, and returns with her to his own hut, the only building on the mine side of the island that was not destroyed by the man's fire.

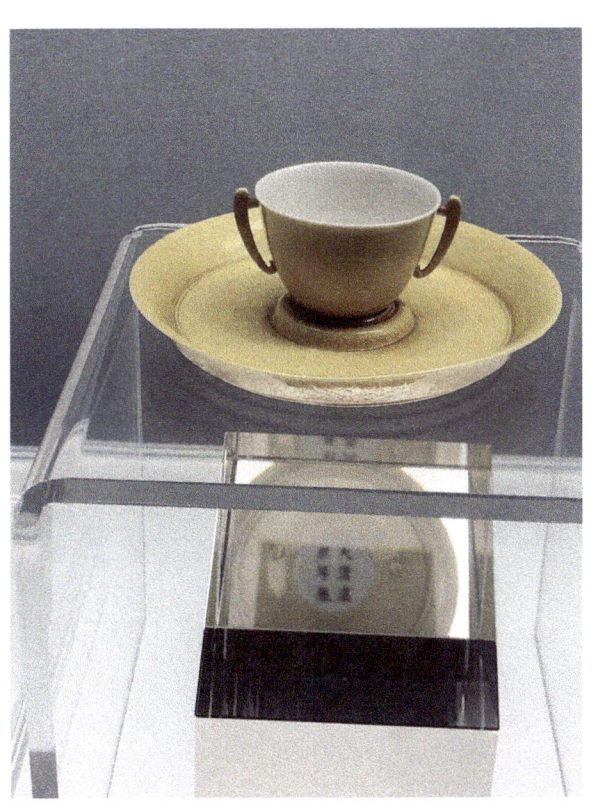

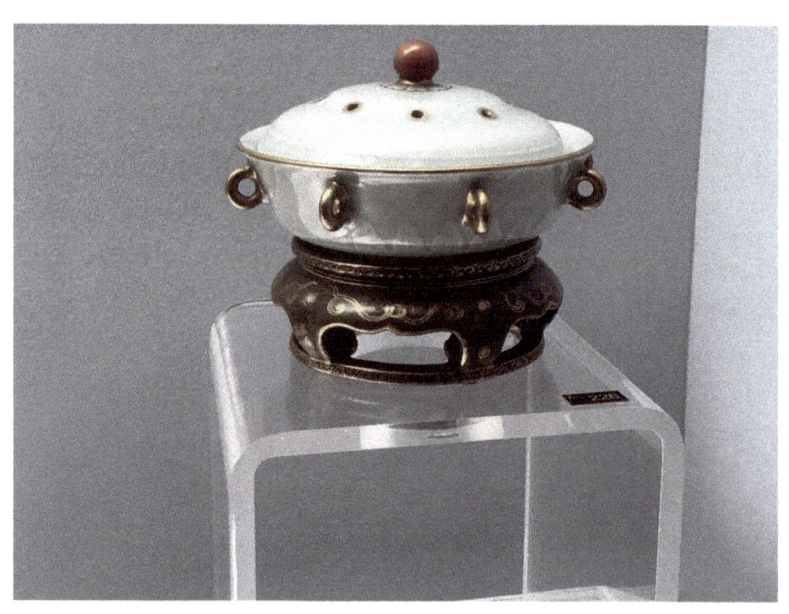

A man who sells vacuum cleaners in a country that is not his own is cornered in the bathroom of a bar by an agent hailing from the country of his birth and asked to provide the country of his birth with secrets on his adopted one. The man has been left by his wife to raise his teenage daughter alone and because the daughter has developed expensive tastes he agrees, adoring the daughter more than anything else. However, he hasn't a clue how to be a spy, and isn't in fact very interested in being one, so when pressed for secrets, he makes them up, choosing agents at random and giving them stories of his own devising. He finds, indeed, he has a flair for the practice, and he makes money on all the agents he creates. The agents of the country of his birth are delighted; they send him a secretary. Then his imaginary agents begin to get killed—or rather, people who fit his agents' descriptions. Worse, his only friend in the country that is not his own, who himself hails from a different country that was recently at war with the country of the man who sells vacuum cleaners' birth, is mysteriously harassed and ultimately killed. This friend, it turns out, had been cornered himself by an agent from the country of his own birth and pressed into providing secrets himself. Thus were the man and his friend forced to spy on one another, despite having no real allegiance to either birth country. Then the man is told by the agents of the country of his birth that he himself is likely to be killed, at a luncheon for salesmen from all these as well as other countries, which these agents view as a mark of success. Instead, a dog is killed. Too many deaths!, the man thinks. He doesn't like it. He finds the man who intended to kill him at the luncheon, a fellow countryman employed by he knows not whom—his home country? the country that is not his own? the country previously at war with his own, or some other?—who also almost certainly killed his friend and shoots him in the doorway of a brothel. Meanwhile, the man has fallen in love with his secretary. Sick with this business of countries and their secrets, he confesses what he's done and is sent back with his daughter and the secretary to the country of his birth.

Because his misdeeds are too embarrassing to reveal, he's given a medal and a job teaching other spies. He and the secretary go off together.

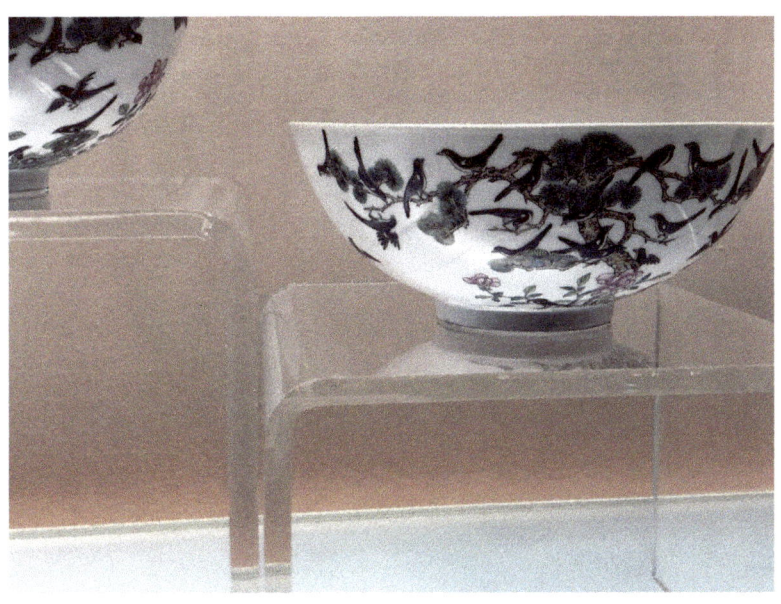

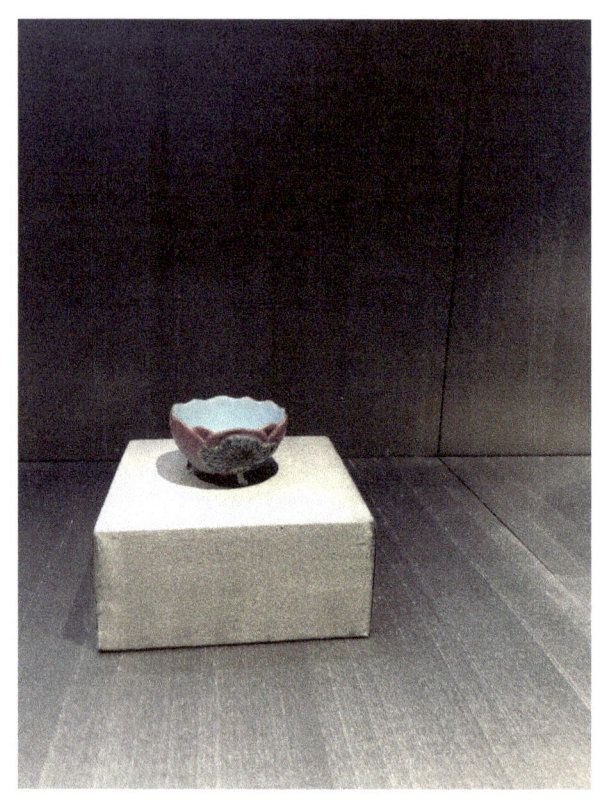

A man finds work on a ship carrying eight hundred religious travelers on a sea very far from the country of his birth. One night, the ship is damaged and begins to fill with water. The captain and two additional crew members lower a boat to save themselves, abandoning both the religious travelers and their crew. At the last minute, the man leaps from the ship to join them in their boat. Later, when they reach the port, they learn that the ship and its passengers were saved by a ship from another country's navy. The captain and the two additional crew members flee and the man, who doesn't understand why he did what he did given his longing for heroism and adventure, is put on trial and stripped of his certification as a seaman. After this, he wanders from port to port, doing well in each job he happens to find until the story of his cowardice resurfaces and hounds him. A sympathetic onlooker arranges a job for him in a village on a remote and commercially insignificant island, far from any port, among people of a different race. Here, he wins the adoration of the people for defending them against a local bandit as well as against the corruptions of their leader. A young woman of their race as well as his falls in love with him. One day, while the man is away in the interior of the island, the village is beset by a marauder from elsewhere. The man returns and negotiates the marauder's departure, but he is betrayed by the stepfather of the mixed race woman, who resents the attention the man has received in the village and offers the marauder an alternate means of escape. The marauder then ambushes the village guards, killing many, including one of the man's close friends. The man's servant then kills the mixed race woman's step-father as he is trying to get off the island. The villagers, when they learn of the massacre, erupt into wails of grief and sorrow. The mixed race woman urges the man to fight but he tells her there is nothing to fight for, and in any case the marauders have gone. She urges him to flee but he says there is no escape. Then he goes, unarmed, to see his dead friend's father to essentially claim responsibility for the death. The father, rising to his feet with the support of two others, shoots the man in the chest and kills him.

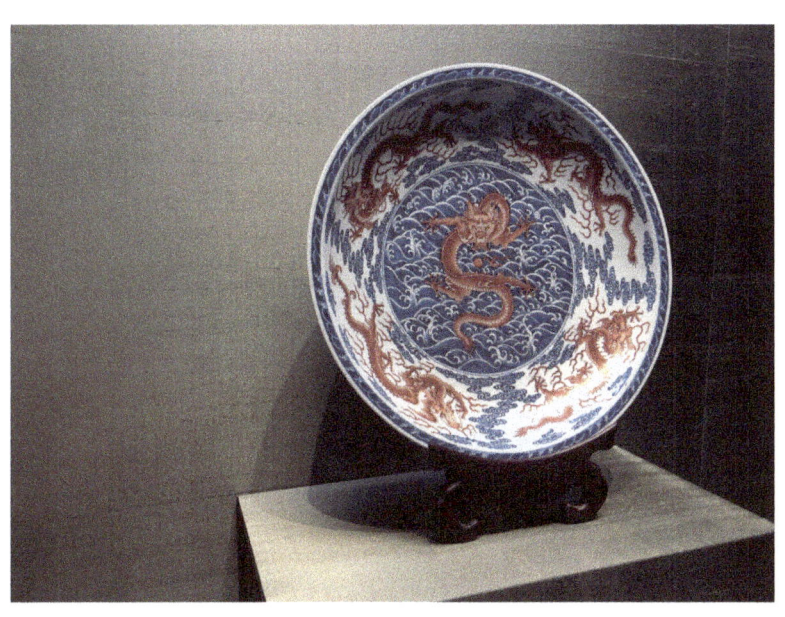

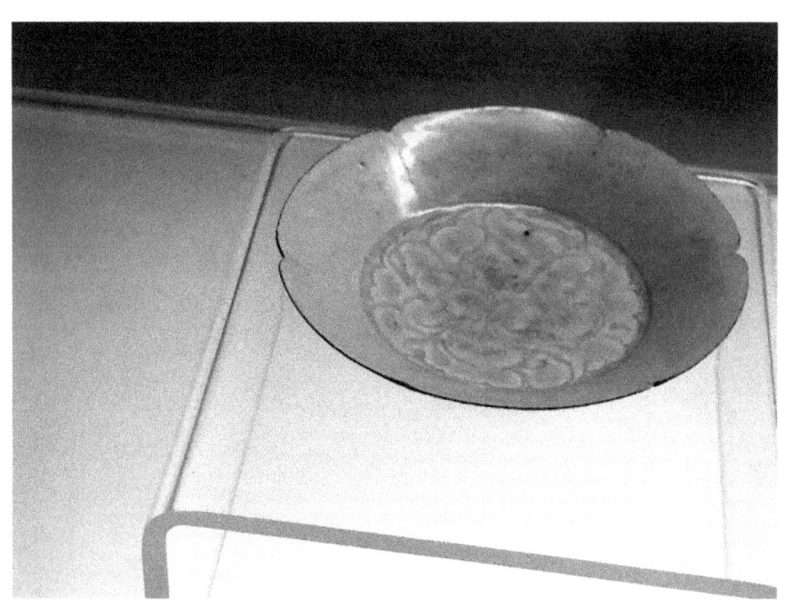

A man working as a journalist in a country very far from his own meets a younger man working as an undercover agent. The two come from different countries, though they share a language, which is different from the language of the country they are in. The man working as a journalist is world-weary and cynical. The younger man is green and idealistic, and the country he's from is on the rise, rapidly eclipsing the other man's country as a global power in the modern age. The man working as a journalist lives with a very young woman of a race native to the country where they are, though he cannot marry her because he is already married. The very young woman's sister disapproves of the relationship and wants her to marry someone better for the family. The man goes to another part of the country to cover a battle. The younger man follows him to confess that he too has fallen in love with the very young woman. After returning from the battle, the man receives an order from his boss to return immediately to his home country. The two men ask the very young woman to choose between them; she chooses to remain with the older man, unaware that he has been ordered home. The man writes to his wife to ask for a divorce. The two men find themselves together again at the site of another battle, trapped in a guard tower. The younger man saves the older man's life. Upon returning, the man tells the very young woman that his wife has agreed to divorce him. The younger man exposes this statement as a lie and the very young woman moves in with him. The man receives new orders from his boss that he is to stay in the country after all. Then a car bomb explodes in the city where they live, killing many innocent people. The man determines that the younger man was involved in the bombing, though he can't expose it in his paper for political reasons. Instead, the man assists in arranging the younger man's murder, after which the very young woman returns to him. Unaware of all that has transpired, the man's wife writes from home to agree to the divorce and the man arranges to bring the very young woman home with him to his own native country.

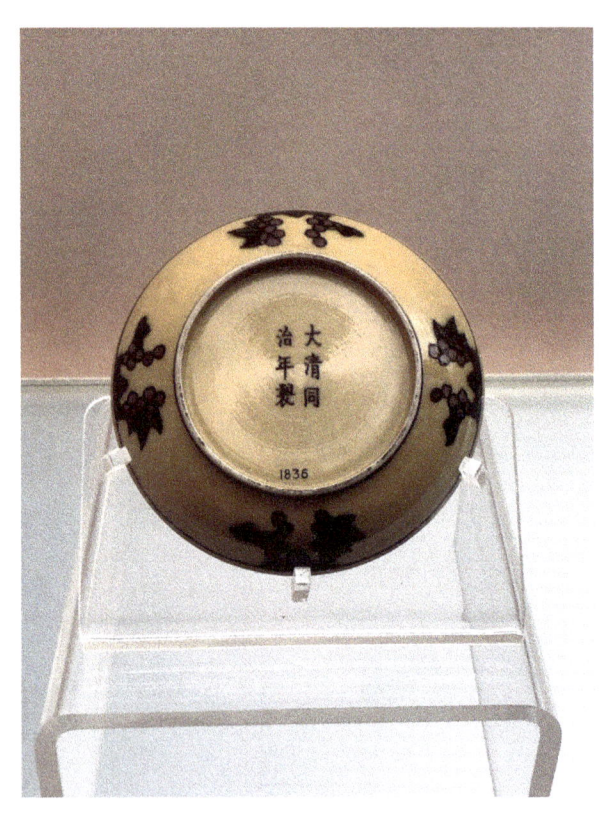

A man who was born and raised in a country very far from the country of his forbearers is taken in, in his youth, by an adventurous and very successful and trader. The trader, who also hails from the country of the man's forbearers and has himself been away from it for a very long time, has an adopted daughter of another race, a race indigenous to the country where they all now are, whom he retrieved as a child from under a pile of dead bodies on a pirate ship in a battle in which her entire community was killed. The trader sends her off to be raised in a convent, where she grows up believing that she is the trader's slave and destined to one day become his wife, which, in accordance with the ethos of her own people, she basically accepts. Instead, the trader marries her off to the man he has taken in, with promises of untold riches to come. It is a miserable marriage. The woman has no respect for the man, and the man, who is only in it for the riches, fears the woman and her strange and furious ways. The marriage produces a daughter, however, and the man loves the daughter inordinately. The man settles with his family in a village on a river where he is the only one of his race, intending to become a trader himself. He sends his daughter off to be raised among others of his own race on a nearby island, but she is met there with unconcealed bigotry and resentment and comes to reject altogether that side of her heritage. Meanwhile, the trader disappears. Once the man loses the ostensible protection of his father-in-law, he is handily usurped by another trader in the village, whose forbearers come from a whole other country. The man is tolerated in the village but, being so obviously a failure, is viewed with contempt by the village leaders and only really relied upon to help facilitate the trafficking of gunpowder under the nose of officials from the country of the man's forbearers, who believe they're in control in this place, and whom the villagers consider ignorant, though dangerous. The man lives in a shack alongside a much grander house that he undertook building in brighter days but never finished and that now sits rotting. The man's daughter returns, grown up and very beautiful. The man continues to believe he will one day secure his riches in the form of gold treasure hidden somewhere up the river, and that he will journey with his daughter to the country of his forbearers, where he has never been, to prove his worth among his own people. Then a young man appears—the son of a king from a nearby island, of a race indigenous to the place where they are, like the mother and most of the villagers—on a ship with a crew in search of gunpowder. The young man immediately falls in love with the daughter, and she falls in love with him. They meet secretly in canoes in the early hours and make plans to return to his island together, which the mother, hating her husband and his people, supports. At the same time, the young man agrees to help the man find his treasure. Before he can do so, however, he runs into trouble with the officials from the country of the man's forbearers, who discover his illegal (by their rules) possession of gunpowder, which explodes and kills two of the officials' men. The young man returns to the village under the cover of night to retrieve the daughter before returning home. A headless corpse has washed up on the bank of the river and the village leaders put the young man's jewelry on the corpse to convey the impression that the young man is dead, which the man himself believes at first. Certain then that he's lost all hope of obtaining his riches, the man grows hopelessly drunk while entertaining the officials who've come to look for the young man, and refuses at first to give them any answers. Then he shows them the corpse, which is in his yard. Only after they've gone does he learn that the young man lives and has escaped with his daughter to a hiding place down the river, where they are waiting on transport to be provided by the village leaders. This is a deeper loss even than the loss of his riches—it is the loss of his one redeeming aspect: his love, and the loss of all his foolish hopes; he is devastated. Meanwhile, a servant girl, who is also in love with the young man, though unrequitedly, has gone around the village screaming that the young man still lives, alerting the officials. The man goes to the place where the young man and his daughter are hiding and threatens at first to hand them over to the officials. At the last minute, however, he helps them to escape. They paddle down the river through the night and stop, come dawn, on an island near the mouth of the river to await the boat that will take them to the young man's island. There, the daughter reveals to the man that, though she does love him, she was cruelly treated at the hands of his people and has no interest claiming any part of his heritage, much less in returning to the country of his forbearers. He swears he will never forgive her. She and the young man leave on a boat. The man returns to the village to find his compound empty, as his wife has moved in with the village leaders. He burns down the shack and moves into the grander, rotting house, where he lives out his days smoking opium with another man who's also the only one of his own race in the village, who's also very far from the country of his forbearers, in a state of irrelevant, heartbroken madness until he dies.

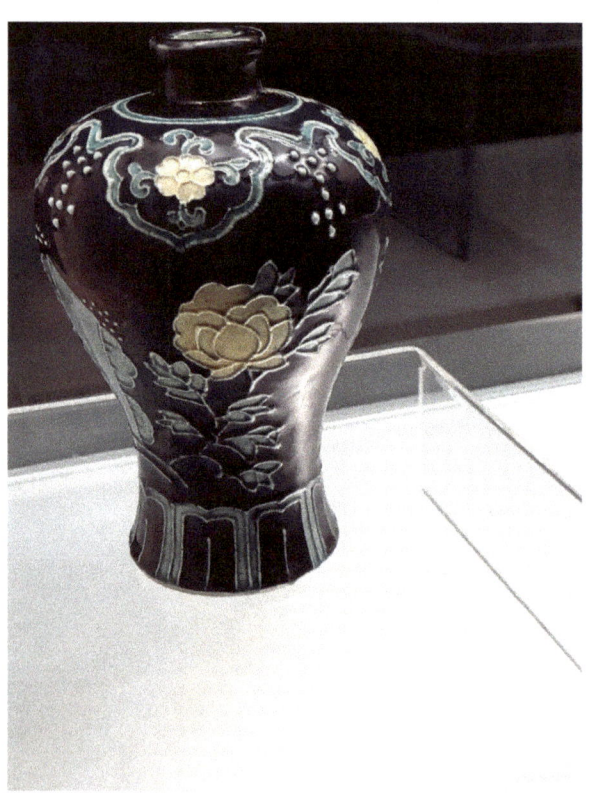

A man who writes adventure novels and has a habit of running into trouble with women travels to a city in a country far from his own to meet an old school friend who has offered him a job. It is a city with an illustrious history that has been devastated in a recent war and divided up, geographically, between four different occupying powers, with a neutral zone at the center. Upon his arrival, the man is mistaken for another, much more talented writer who happens to have the same last name, who is also expected in this city at this time to give a speech to a literary society. Soon after, the man learns that his friend is dead, hit by a car in the street outside his apartment building several days before. He worshiped this friend throughout his youth and weeps at his funeral, which is meagerly attended—just two other men, a detective, and a girl. The detective informs the man over drinks afterward that his friend was actually a shady character, but the man won't believe it and takes a swing at him. The man has no applicable currency, so the detective buys his drinks and gets him a room. At the hotel, however, the man is once again mistaken for the more talented writer and given that writer's room as well as his spending money. The man sets out to clear his friend's name and soon encounters conflicting accounts of his death, causing him to suspect foul play. He seeks out the girl from the funeral, his friend's former girlfriend, who comes from a different country than she claims to come from, and promptly falls in love with her. As he begins to unravel the plot against his friend, he is picked up off the street in a car carrying the flag of one of the occupying powers. He believes that he will be arrested or killed, but instead he is delivered to a room full of elderly strangers to give the speech the more talented writer was supposed to give, which confuses everybody. Eventually, the man learns that his friend wasn't killed at all but faked his own death to get out of trouble. The crime for which he is wanted by the detective was indisputably immoral and horrific, and the man, in learning of it, is forced to reckon his lifelong admiration for his friend against his own conscience as a decent if somewhat naïve individual.

In the end, he goes with his conscience and turns on his friend, conspiring with the detective to apprehend him. Sensing a trap, the friend escapes and leads the man and the detective on a chase through the city's network of sewers. The friend shoots at the man and instead kills one of the detective's officers. The man shoots at the friend, injuring him, then, after a bit of a chase through the dark, shoots again, killing him. The friend's last words are enigmatic: they may be a curse on the man for his naivete or they may be a faltering act of contrition. (Probably the former.) The man and the detective meet one last time at the friend's second funeral, and the man goes off with the friend's former girlfriend.

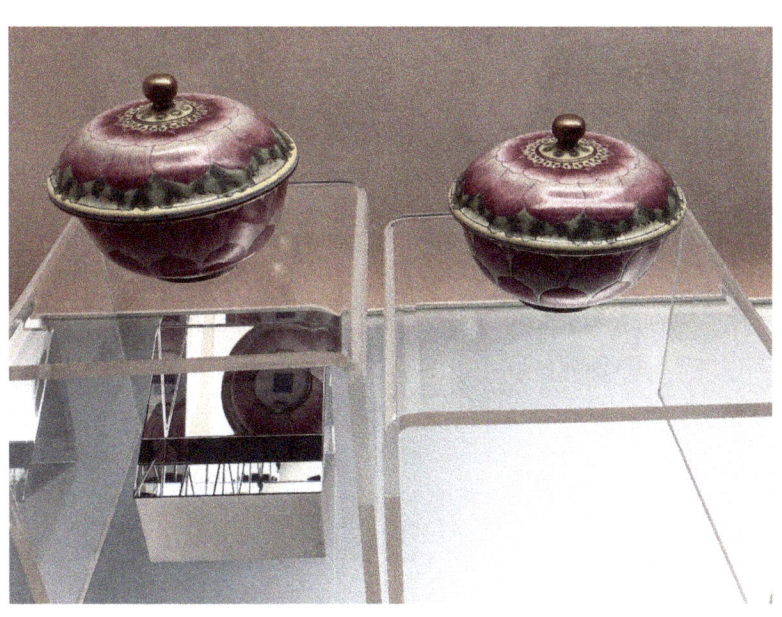

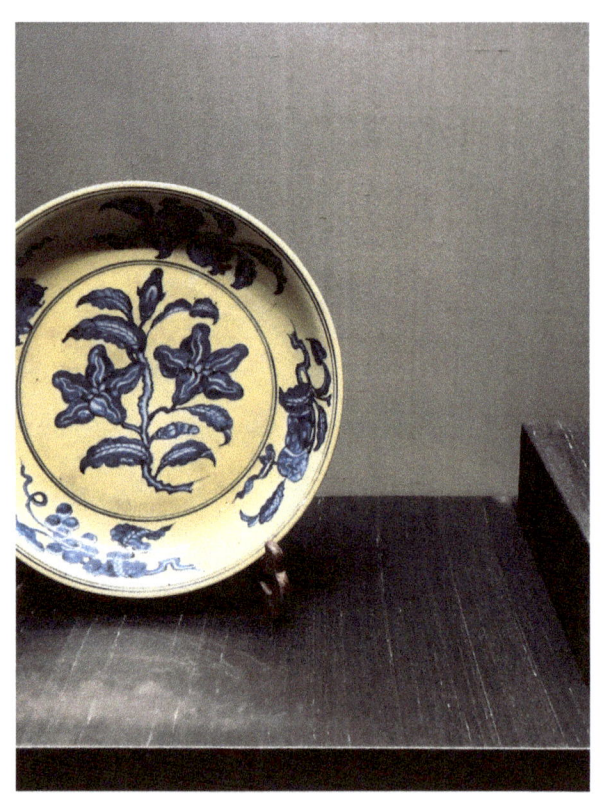

A man who was abducted from boarding school, more or less willingly, at the age of twelve by a mysterious grifter who claims that he won the boy from his father in a backgammon game is raised in the home of the grifter's mistress, who has always wanted a child of her own. In fact, she would have had a child of her own, years before, by the man's own father had the father not pressured her into an abortion, and had not the doctor so bungled the job. The mistress becomes a surrogate mother to the man, while the grifter appears only intermittently, giving little indication of where he goes when he's gone or how he lives. The father appears periodically as well, dropping vague threats and shadowy allusions, but never attempts to take his son back. The man is intrigued by these characters but doesn't love them, and feels some guilt for his lack of gratitude. Eventually, he moves out and becomes a journalist. When later the mistress is admitted to the hospital with serious injuries following an accident, the man finds letters from the grifter in her possession from an address in a country very far from their own, with a check and a plea to the mistress to join him. Knowing the mistress will never make it, the man cashes his check and flies there himself. He is met by someone who calls himself a journalist, who claims to hail from the man's own country, though speaks with the accent of a different country, and is given a bodyguard by the military leader of the town. The grifter appears after a couple of days, but the man can't bring himself to tell him that the mistress has died. It is unclear, in this place, who's on whose side. The grifter is known to own a small airplane, which he employs in transporting illicit goods for one side or another of a guerilla war. The so called journalist who speaks with the wrong accent, who claims to be neutral but probably isn't, tries to win the man over by offering him a job, which the grifter strongly discourages him from taking. The military leader also attempts to gain the man's confidence, to get information out of him concerning the grifter. When the man finally tells the grifter that the mistress has died, he becomes enraged and wants nothing more to do with the man, forsaking him as a surrogate son. Then he dies in a suicide mission in his airplane, a mission that turns out to have had a false target, in which no one is killed but the grifter himself. The man takes the money the grifter left behind to embark on his own adventure in this new country, but dies in a car accident on his way to the airport, leaving behind a manuscript account of this whole story in a waste basket in the hotel. After he's gone, the military leader and the so called journalist who speaks with the wrong accent meet to ponder the evidence the man left behind, believing the manuscript to be filled with codes.

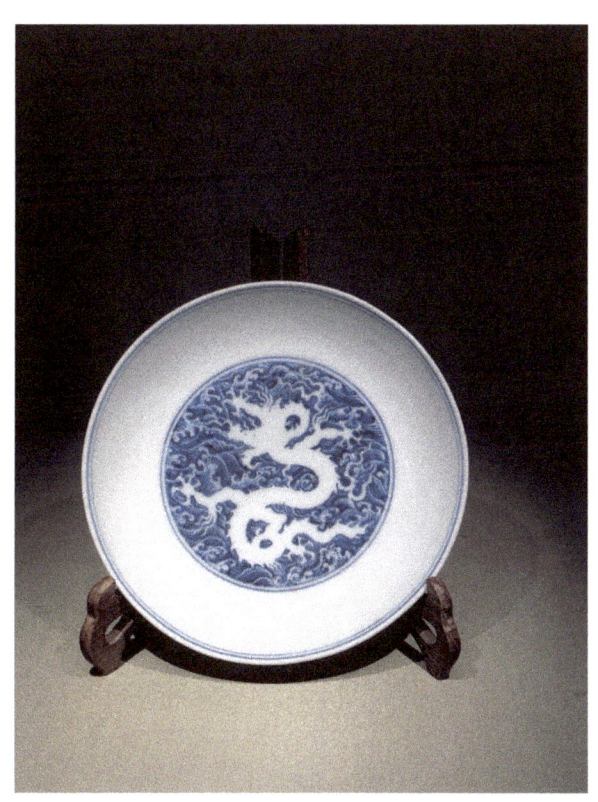

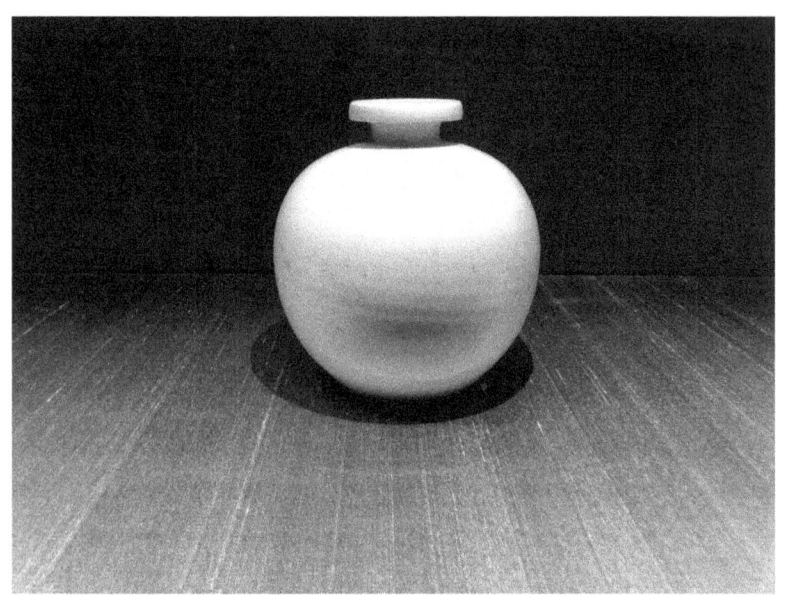

A man with a calm, unflappable nature, whose sole act of imagination or daring was to run off to sea at the age of fifteen, is captain of a ship that is sailing in a sea very far from the country of his birth when the barometer suddenly takes a dive. The ship carries cargo as well as two hundred migrant workers of a different race, who speak a different language, returning home after years of working abroad. The man, though well into a long and respected career, has never experienced a true calamity at sea, and he determines to sail into the storm head on. First, the air is still and hot, with large, inexplicable swells in the sea. Then, after nightfall, the wind comes up and the sea begins to dash the ship with a ferocious, almost personal animosity. This goes on for six hours. All is dark and the crew can scarcely hear one another in the din, even when screaming into one another's face. The migrants are locked up in a room below deck. There, the chests containing their hard-earned wages are smashed and the migrants nearly tear one another to pieces trying to get hold of their own silver dollars, as the lurching of the ship tosses them to and fro and they are bruised and lacerated by the flying debris. The sight of this melee horrifies the crew members and most would prefer to leave the migrants locked up. At the captain's insistence, however, they are eventually released. After six hours, the winds suddenly cease and for twenty minutes, near dawn, the sea is calm. Then the ship enters into the second half of the storm. It arrives in port, in the end, looking like something dredged up from under the sea. The captain, along with the migrants' translator, pacifies a potential revolt by the migrants by collecting all their lost silver dollars and dividing the dollars equally between them. The captain writes home to his wife, describing the storm, but the wife, who cares for her husband well enough in the abstract but actually dreads the day he will retire and come home, barely reads the letter, and misses altogether the passage in which he admits to having feared for his life. Then she takes her daughter shopping, assuring all who ask that her husband is well and that the climate in the sea where he is sailing agrees with him.

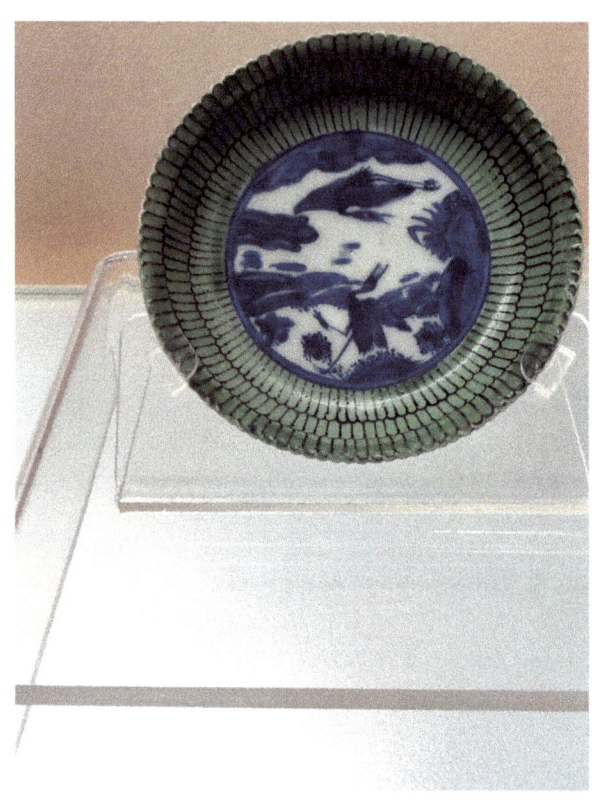

A man who lives on the coast of a country very far from his own, married to a woman whom he pities but does not love, is denied a promotion his wife had been hoping for. The wife is very unhappy in this country. Their only child has died long ago and she has no friends, save a besotted young colleague of her husband whose professed love she does not return. She asks the man to move her to another country. He is willing but cannot afford it. He applies for a loan but his application is denied. There is a war going on in the man and his wife's own country, which is very far from both the country where they live and the country where his wife wants to go, and he is charged with inspecting passing ships for smuggled cargo and suspicious communications. He finds a letter in the possession of the captain of a ship from a country with which his own country is at war and he seizes it; the captain tries to bribe him but the man refuses. He later reads the letter and finds that it's harmless, merely a personal letter to the captain's daughter. He destroys it. Then the man journeys inland, to another post, to deal with the suicide of another young inspector who'd fallen into debt with a smooth-talking black marketer who hails from yet another country. When confronted about the death of the inspector, the black marketer offers the man a loan that would cover his wife's passage to her new country; first he denies it, then he accepts. The wife leaves. The man's post is then beset by the survivors of a shipwreck, including a young girl, now orphaned, who dies in his charge, and a young woman, now widowed, who reminds him of his long dead daughter. He begins a passionate affair with the widow, an act that, because he is a religious man, he believes to be a grave sin. The black marketer gets his hands on a letter the man has written to the widow and blackmails him into smuggling diamonds. The man's wife returns. The man does not confess his sin either to his wife or to his priest, nor does he renounce the affair. The man's servant observes him in an embrace with the widow, and the man, concerned that the servant will betray him, tells the black marketer he believes the servant is disloyal. The black marketer has the servant killed. The man is subsumed with guilt for both the affair and the death. Though he believes suicide to be the ultimate sin, he fakes a heart attack and kills himself with pills. Another man tries to make love to the widow, who's now lost her husband and her lover in close succession, but she is inert on the bed, says she can't love anyone. The besotted young colleague returns to the wife, who knew of the affair all along, it turns out, and implores her to marry him; she puts him off. She comes to see that the death was a suicide—the gravest of sins in her and her husband's faith—and wonders aloud to her priest how the man could have made such a mess of things.

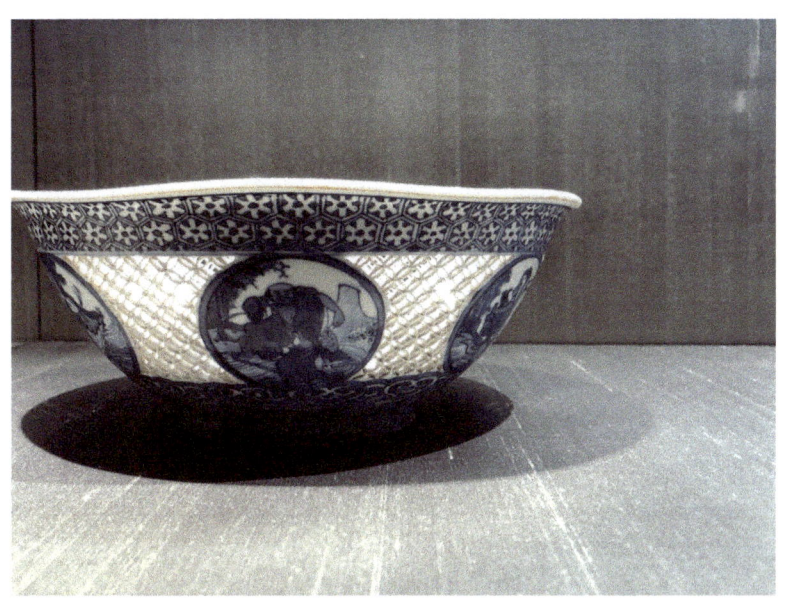

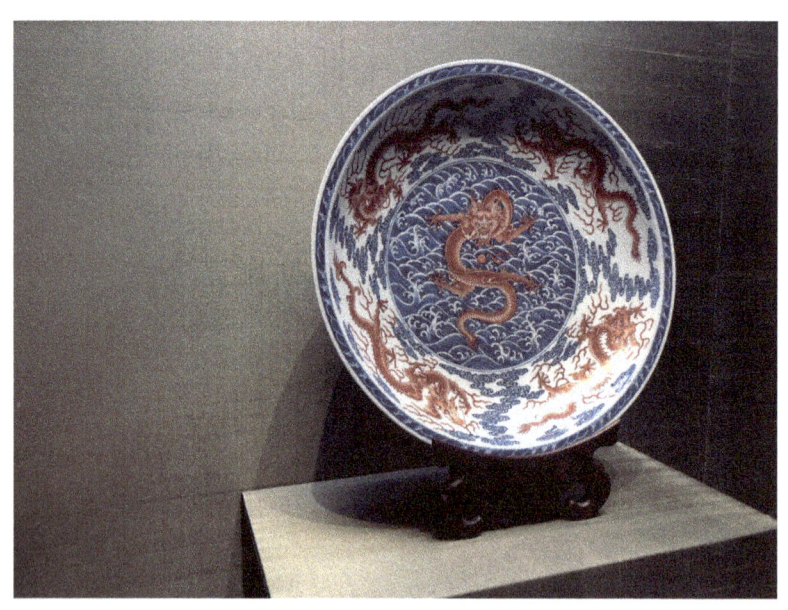

A man who was born very poor and raised on the sea from the age of twelve returns to the country of his birth as an old man, with a fortune in gold pieces sewn into his clothes. The country is just then emerging from a bloody revolution in which he had no part and took no side, belonging himself, in his view, to no nation at all but to an international brotherhood of piratical seamen. He rents a room on the end of a peninsula with windows to the sea on three of four sides and lives there in peace for eight years. Also living in the house are a wild-eyed young woman whose parents were killed in front of her during the bloody revolution, the young woman's somber aunt, and a fanatical partisan whose cause, though initially triumphant, is gradually losing hold in this country. The old man buys from the partisan a small ship whose hull was at one time filled with dead bodies. He cleans out the hull and restores the ship to a sea worthy state, then parks it in a hidden cove. One day, a soldier appears, also renting a room in the house while on his leave from the government that's succeeded that of the partisan. He returns several times. There is an enemy ship lurking just off the coast, visible from this peninsula, and the soldier and the old man watch its movements. Soon the soldier attempts to recruit the old man in a plan he's been charged with to plant false correspondence in the path of that ship. Unbeknownst, at first, to either of them, the enemy ship dispatches several soldiers in a boat to attempt to make contact with the wild-eyed young woman's parents, whom they believe might provide them with information. They fail to find the parents, who are of course long dead, and are frightened off by the sight of the wild-eyed young woman, though they inadvertently leave one man behind. The old man finds this enemy soldier lurking near his small ship and, aiming to protect his ship, knocks him out with a cudgel and locks him up in the hull. Later, however, he finds that he knows the man from their days of belonging to the international brotherhood, though the enemy soldier, in his concussive daze, doesn't recognize the old man, and believes he's going to be taken prisoner by the government of the country where he has been stranded. While the old man is up at the house, the partisan goes looking for his compatriot soldier with a pitchfork—among other sources of enmity between them, both are in love with the wild-eyed young woman—and stumbles instead on the enemy soldier, who then escapes and locks the partisan in the hull. The enemy soldier is eventually picked up by his compatriots, never learning that the old man was once his friend. The old man and the soldier agree that the soldier will take the small ship and allow himself to be captured by the enemy, along with the false correspondence, though it means an indefinite period of captivity. The soldier volunteers in part because he is afraid of his love for the wild-eyed young woman, believing she is crazy—though in fact, he himself, the young woman and the partisan, all having come of age during the bloody revolution, are all disturbed in their own way. The soldier and the old man go to prepare the ship, but the wild-eyed young woman comes chasing after them, not wanting the soldier to leave. It's raining. She faints onboard the small ship and, while the soldier is carrying her back up to the house, the old man leaves with the ship himself, along with the partisan, who's been tied up on the deck, and a local peasant who helps with the ship. The old man sets out to sea and, as the soldier watches in frustration from the end of the peninsula, leads the enemy ship on a chase that deceives its captain into believing the small ship has something to hide. The old man allows the small ship to be caught. As they approach, the enemy soldiers shoot and kill the old man, the partisan, and the peasant. They capture the small ship and later sink it and the enemy captain brags of the operation to his superior. The soldier and the wild-eyed young woman marry and live out their days in the house on the peninsula. Years later, they find the old man's fortune in gold pieces stuffed into a well.

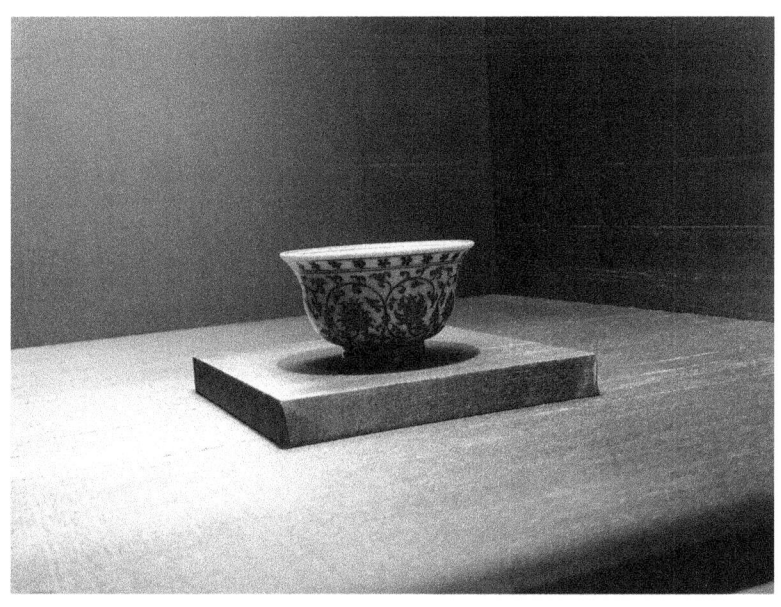

Note: The preceding texts are synopses of novels and stories by Joseph Conrad and Graham Greene. The images were taken in Shanghai and Suzhou, China, which is the farthest place I have been from the place of my birth.

Mapwalkers

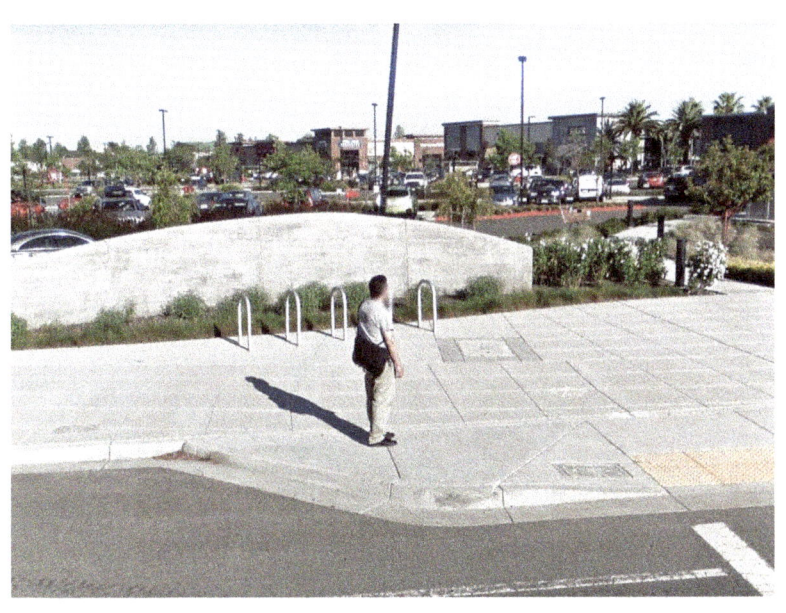

2745 Fifth Street, Alameda, CA

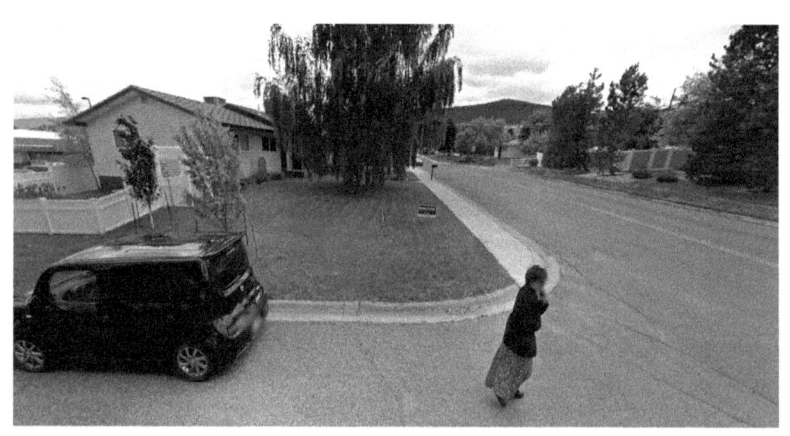

2301 Lockey Avenue, Helena, MT

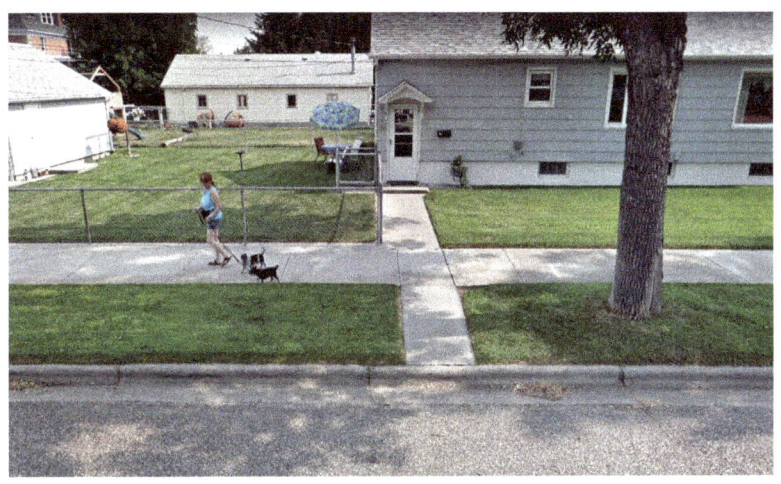

3515 2nd Avenue S., Billings, MT

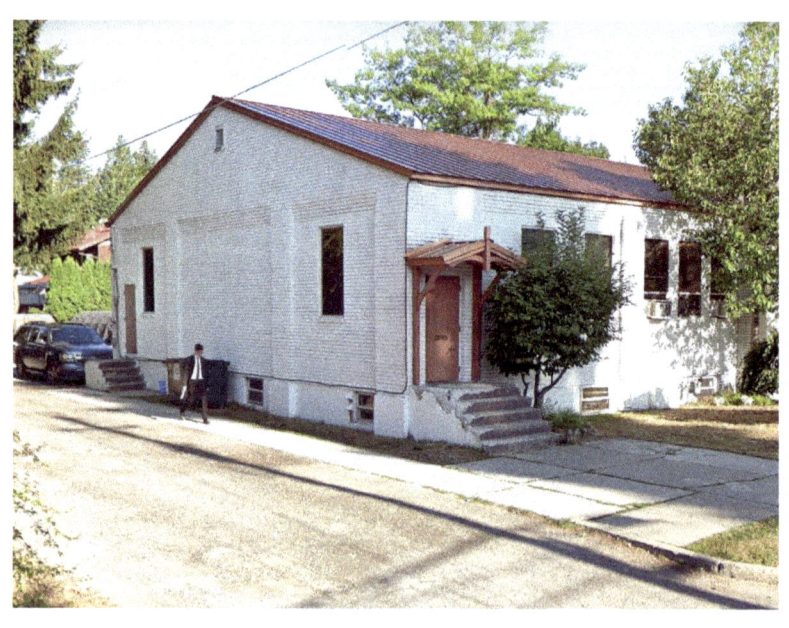

763 N. 11th Street, Couer d'Alene, ID

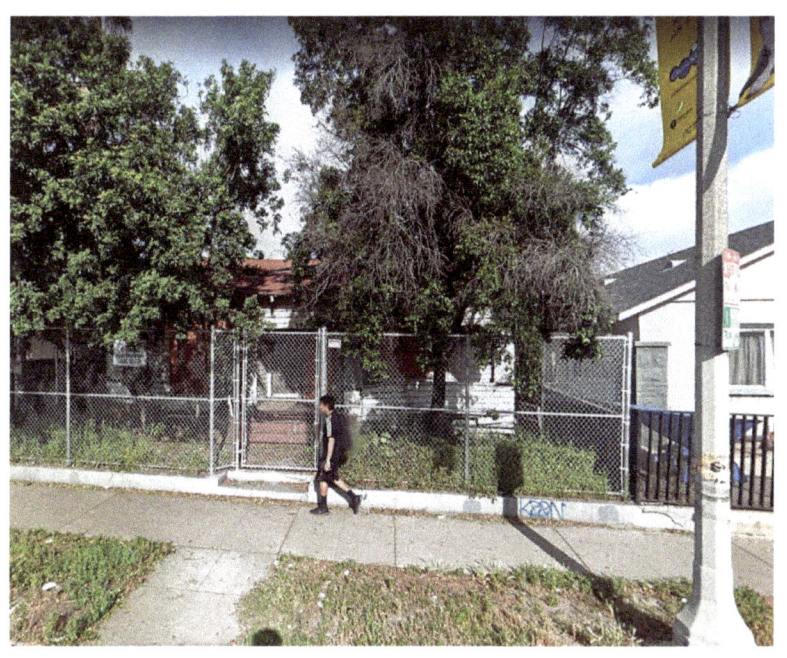

659 S. Soto Street, Los Angeles, CA

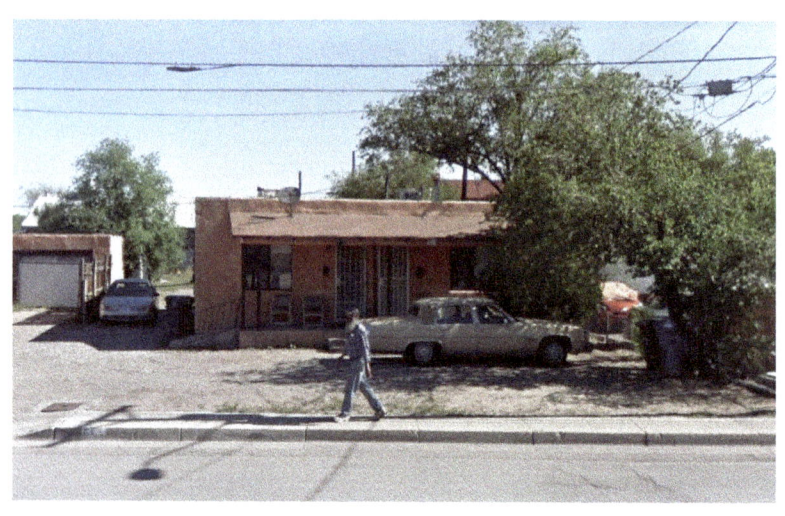

517 Candelaria Road NW, Albquerque, NM

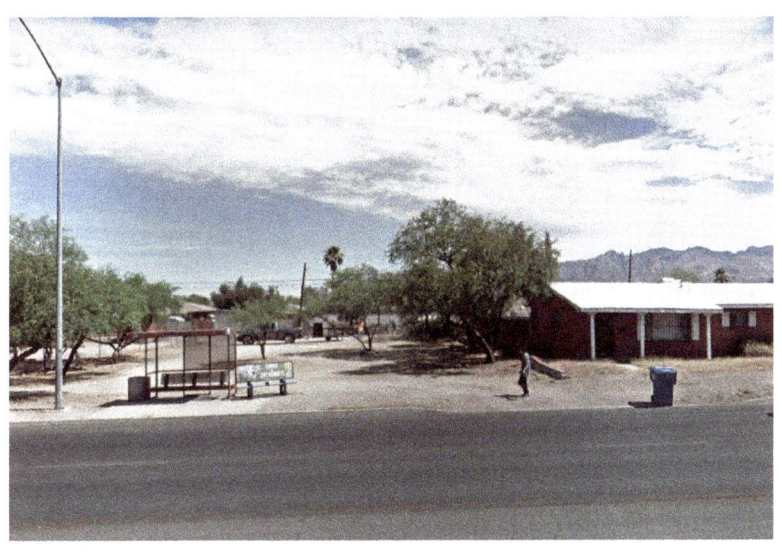

1560 E. Grant Road, Tucson, AZ

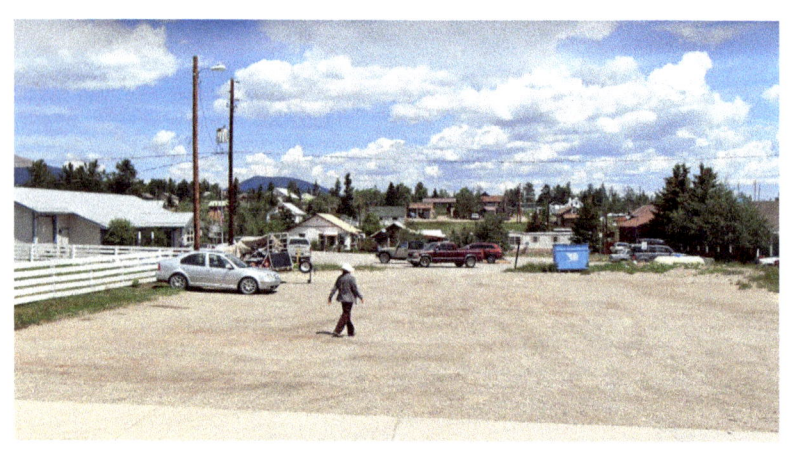

521 Main Street, Fairplay, CO

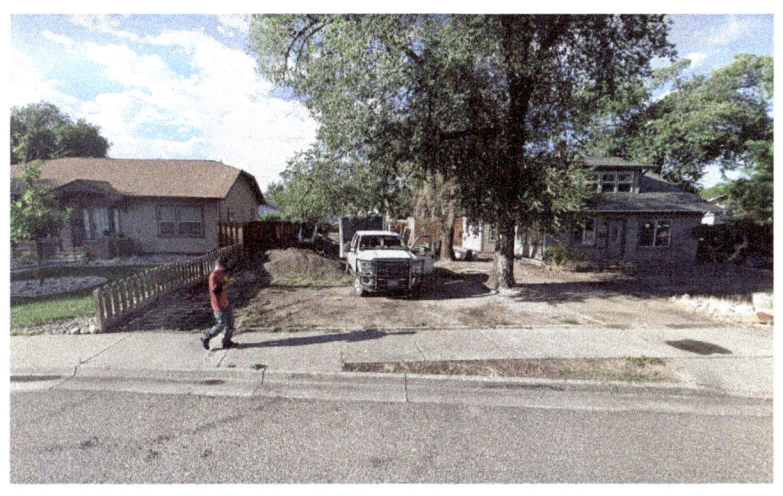

1528 Grand Avenue, Grand Junction, CO

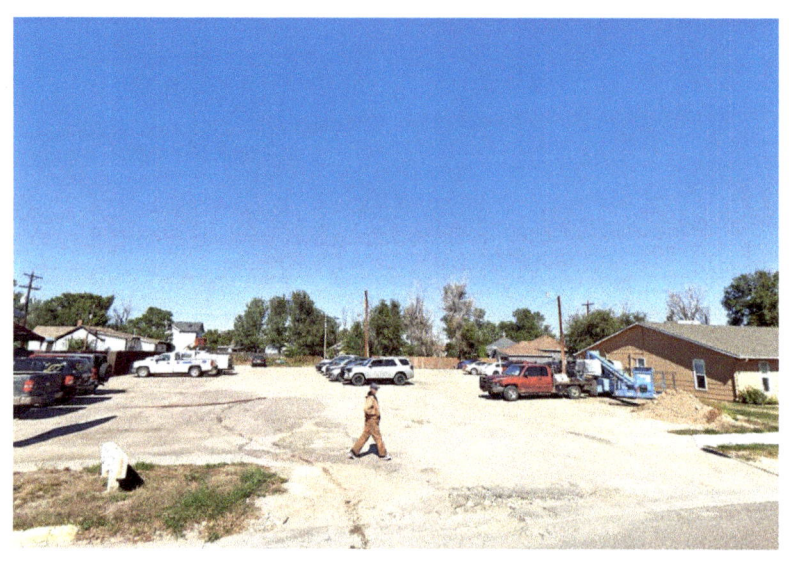

668 U.S.-24, Limon, CO

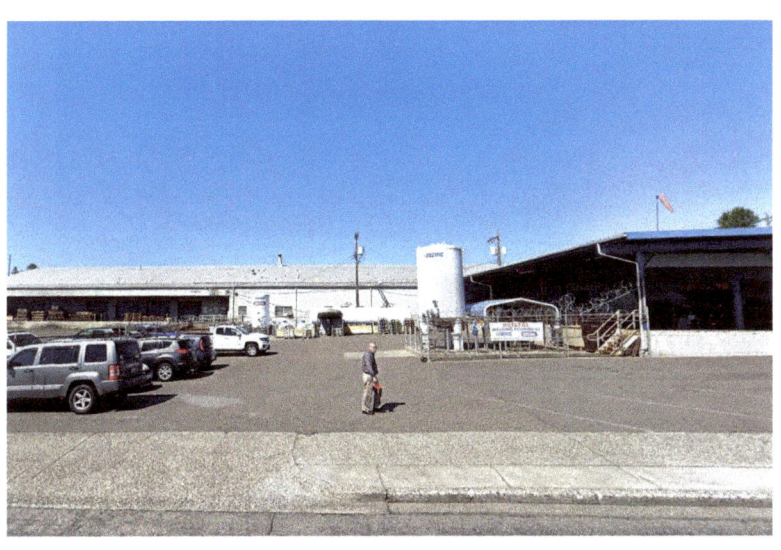

2912 S. M Street, Tacoma, WA

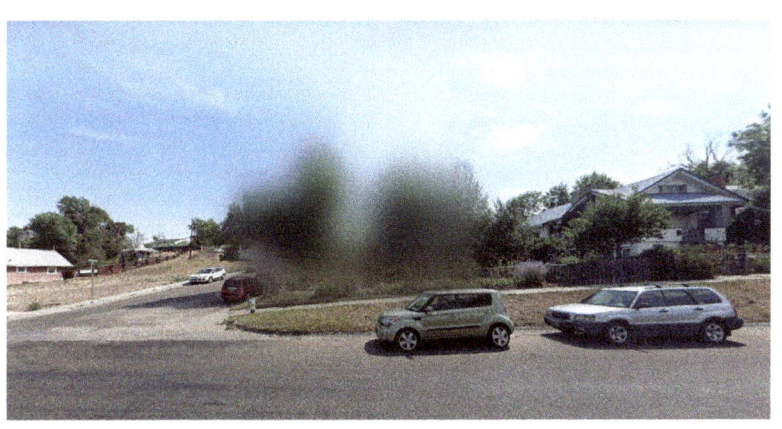

800 S. McKinley Street, Casper, WY

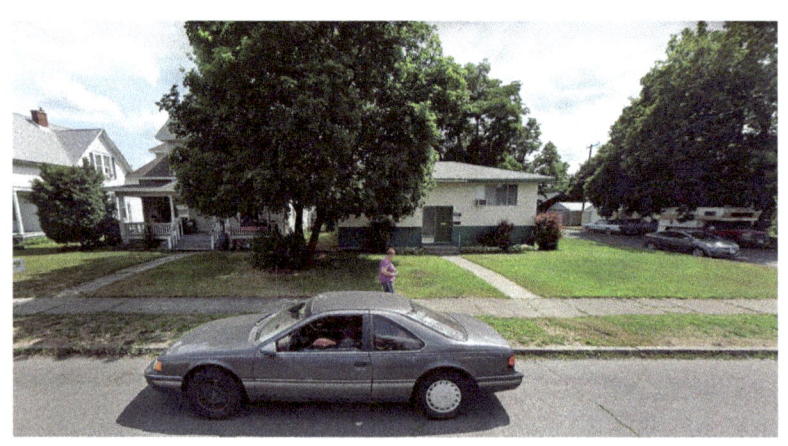

1026 W. Fairview Avenue, Spokane, WA

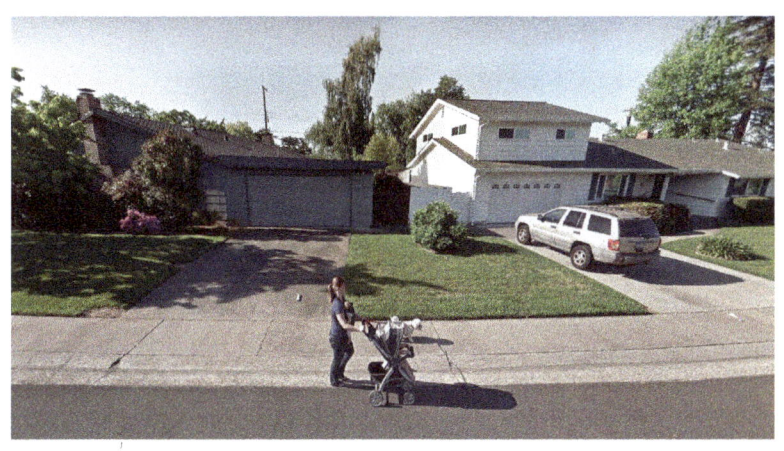

4433 Elizabeth Avenue, Sacramento, CA

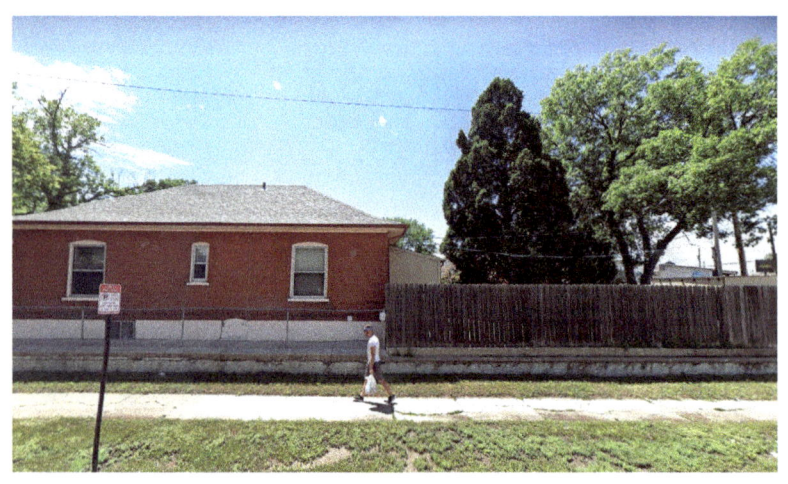

3529 W. 44th Avenue, Denver, CO

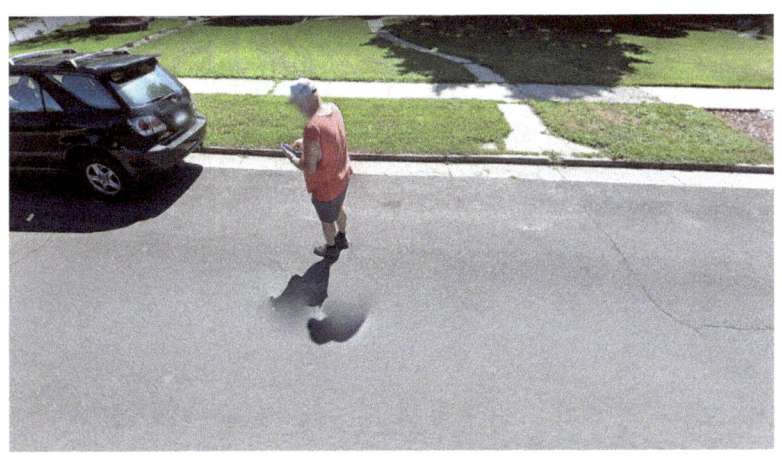

4740 Alcott Street, Denver, CO

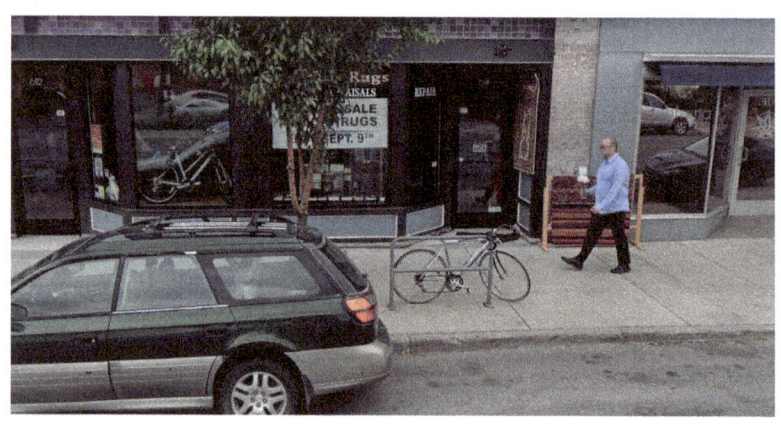

612 S. Higgins Avenue, Missoula, MT

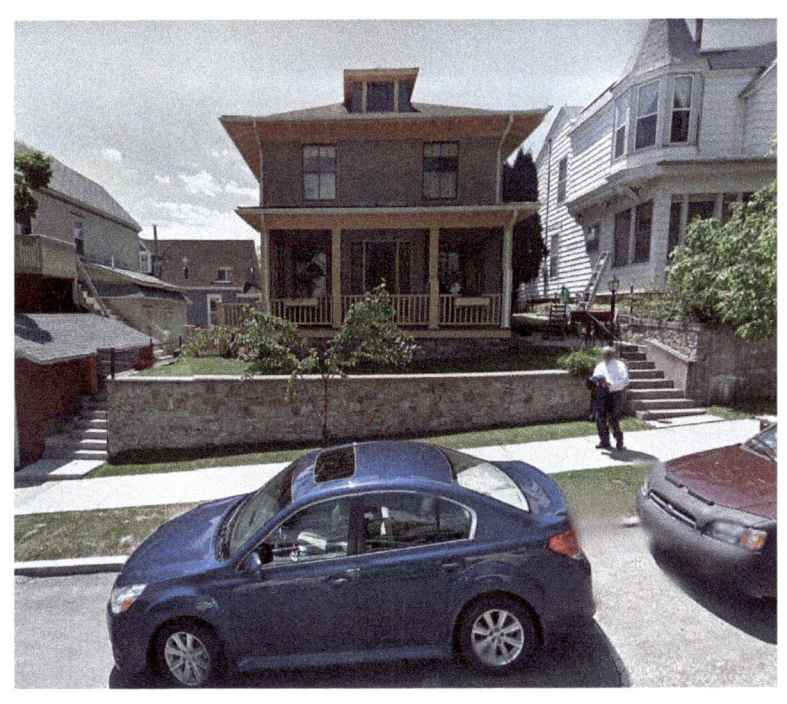

609 Holter Street, Helena, MT

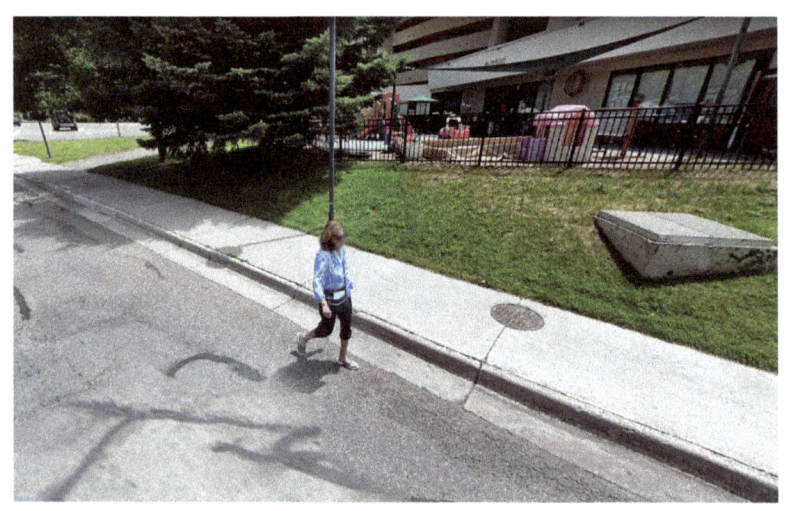

289 Mikaela Way, Avon, CO

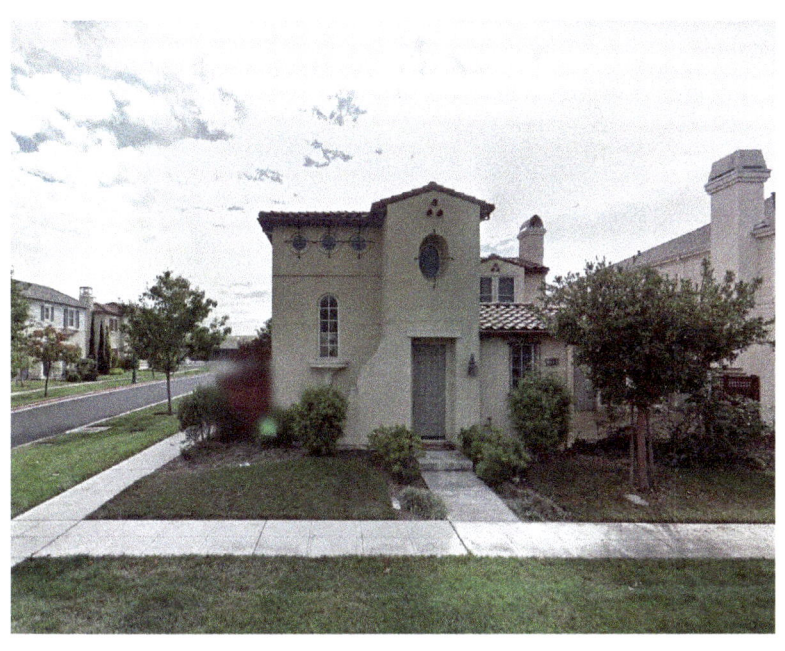

339 Lina Avenue, Alameda, CA

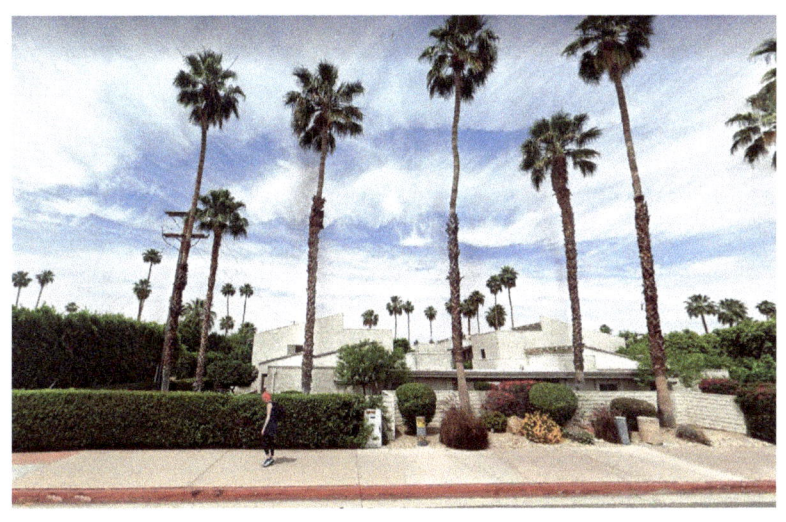

1140 E. Palm Canyon Drive, Palm Springs, CA

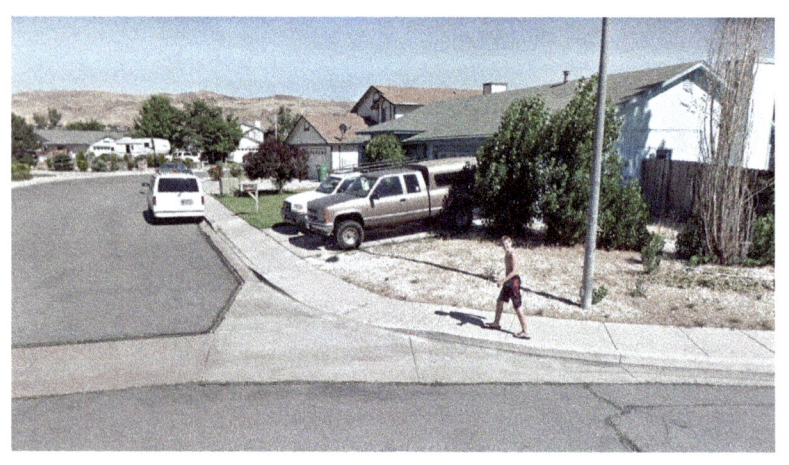

1276 Union Street, Sparks, NV

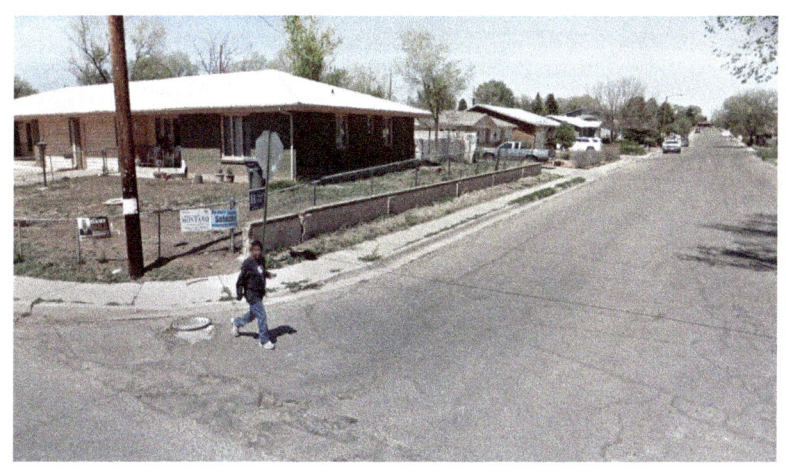

2100 8th Street, Las Vegas, NM

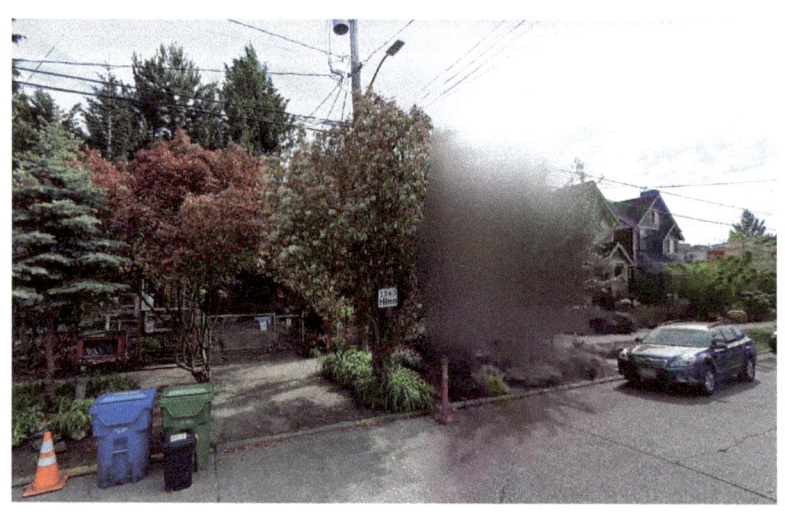

1547 NW 58th Street, Seattle, WA

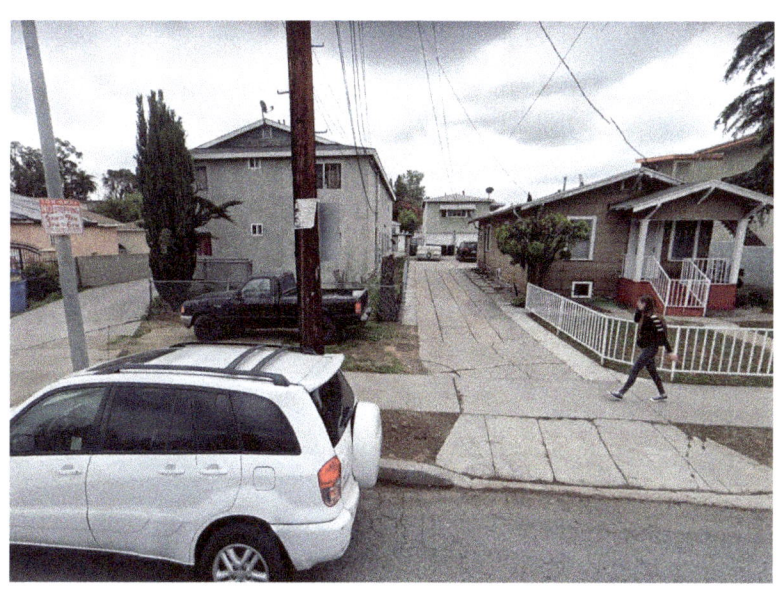

1460 N. Soto Street, Los Angeles, CA

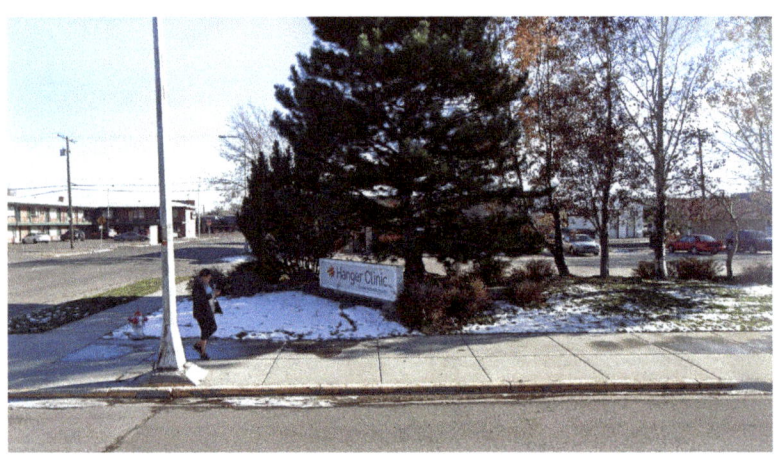

3400 I-90BL, Billings, MT

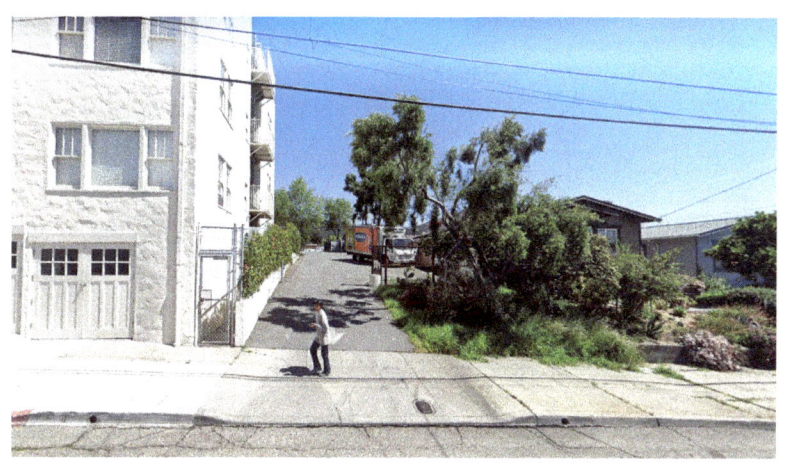

3507 Redding Street, Oakland, CA

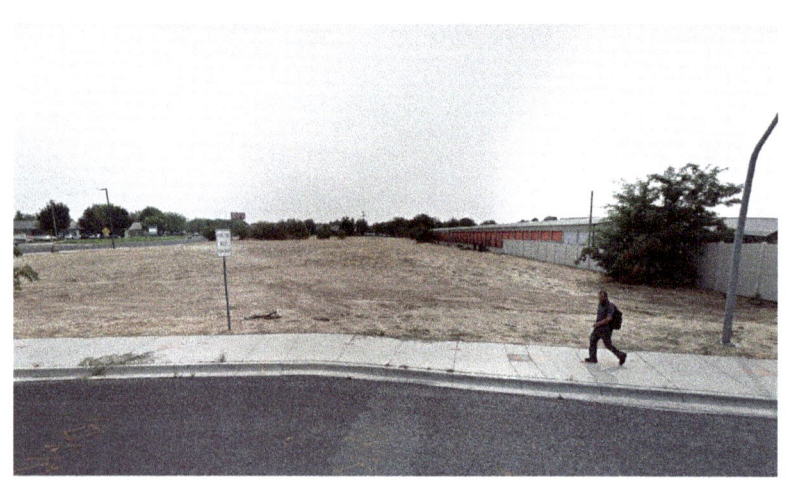

641 N. Maple Grove Road, Boise, ID

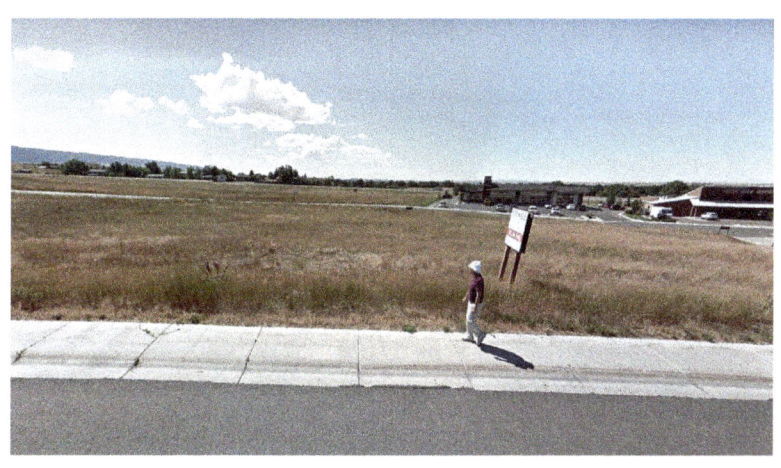

1521 Centennial Hills Boulevard, Casper, WY

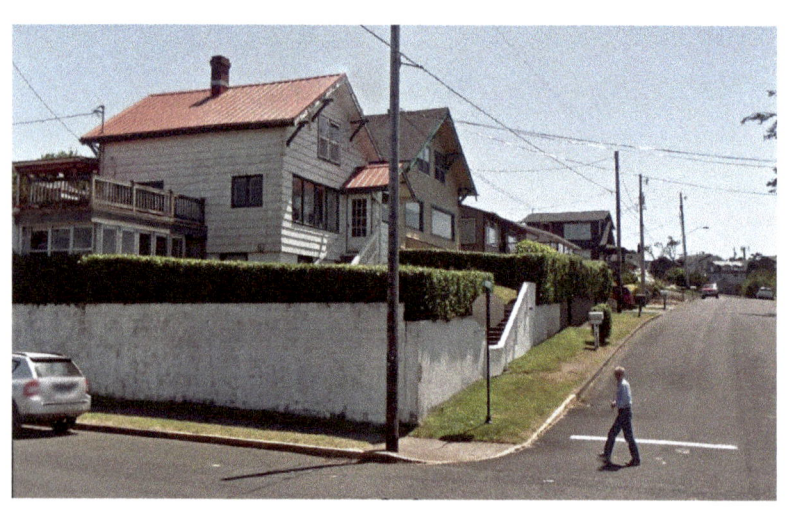

1 NW Hurbert Street, Newport, OR

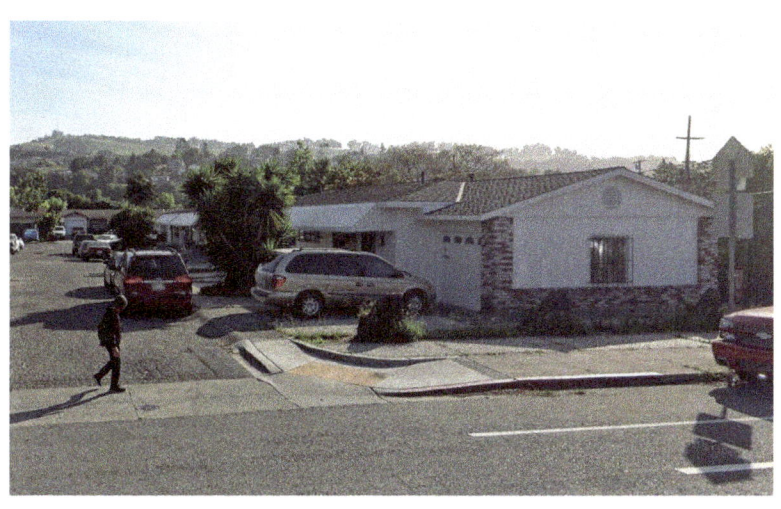

14584 Bancroft Avenue, San Leandro, CA

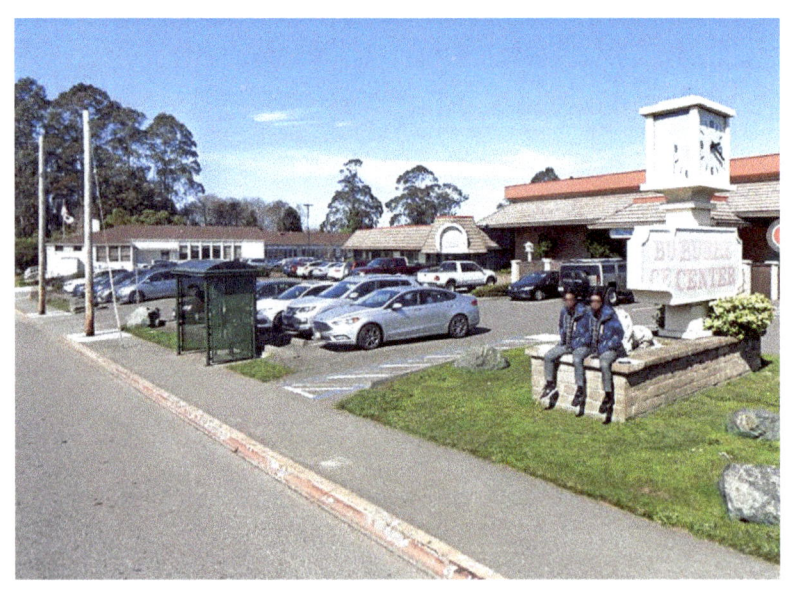

999 Myrtle Avenue, Eureka, CA

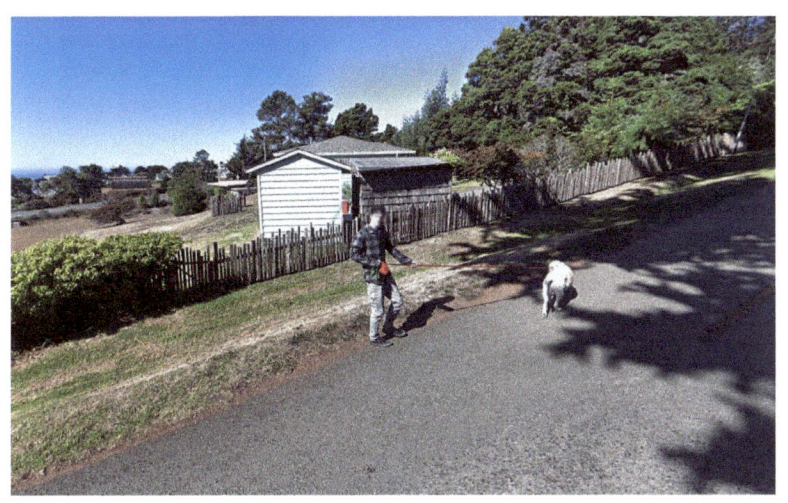

10381 Clark Street, Mendocino, CA

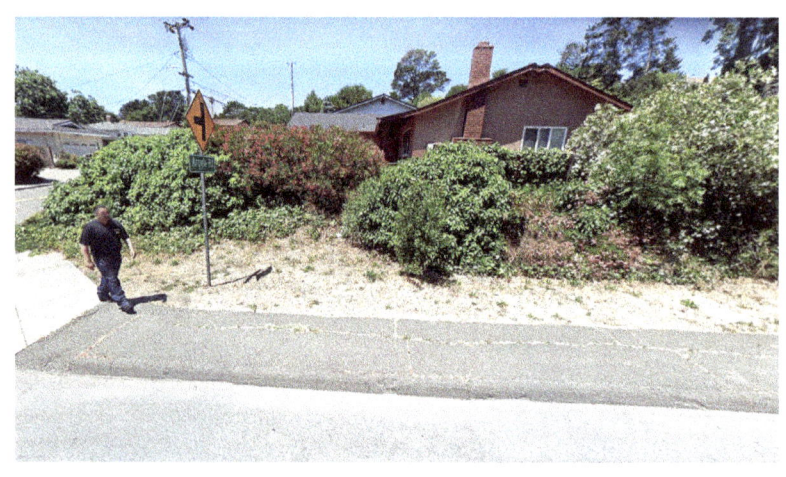

620 Appian Way, El Sobrante, CA

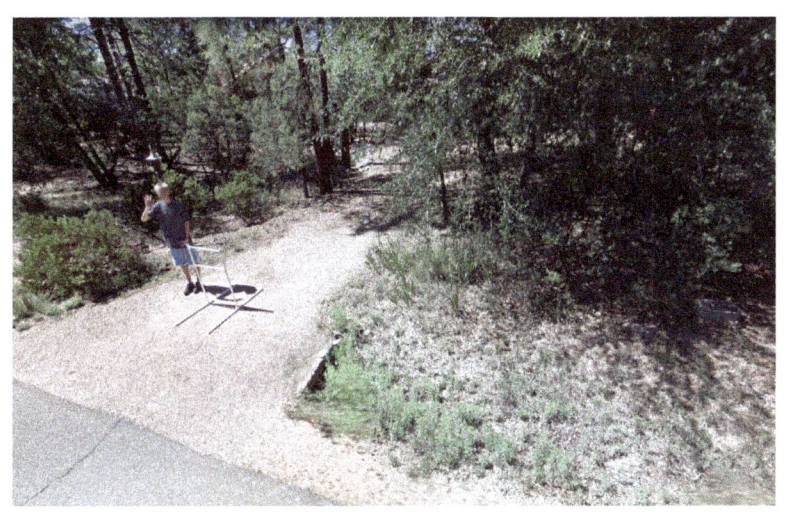

203 W. Holly Circle, Payson, AZ

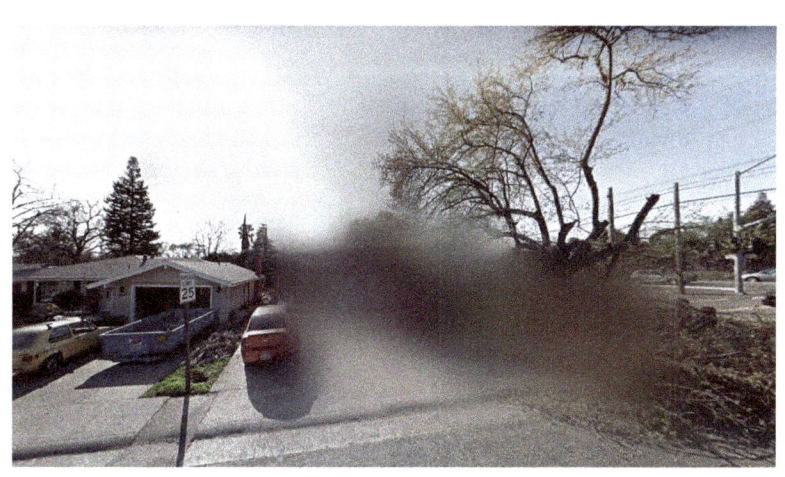

5349 Chicago Avenue, Sacramento, CA

They wander nameless and indistinct, almost incorporeal, like ghosts. Their bodies are shadows against the more solid streets; they have no purpose here. They have no faces. In a photograph, even hazy bystanders have a kind of dignity. One knows that they exist in the flesh—somewhere; or that they did, at some time. Between the lens and the eye there is a natural correspondence that establishes in a photograph, from the outset, a degree of trust. Here, one isn't so sure. They are almost translucent. Where did they come from? Where are they going? There is a peculiar emptiness. Their presence is incidental here, or worse: a blemish on the more stable, the more necessary reality of the map, like a stain across the pages of a magazine.

The world is the world of Google Street View, which is not exactly our world but something like it: a patched together simulacrum intended to convey a perception not of recognition primarily, or association, but of access and mobility. The project involved dropping into cities and towns at random, like a paratrooper, and wandering the streets till I found someone. Sometimes (often) it took quite a while. Touch down in Paris, Tokyo, Mexico City, Bangkok—there are bodies everywhere. The buildings close in familiarly around them; the streets are as narrow as alleys in places. There are sidewalk cafes and scores of motor scooters. There are vendors with carts engaging visibly in commerce. Out here, the streets are wide and arid. The neighborhoods have an air of desertion. There are families, assemblies, crowds, congregations, rallies, mobs somewhere in America, sure, but where? Not out here. Yet, with persistence, eventually: a lone body, walking.

Every map is an act of translation. The overwhelming chaos of three-dimensional space is distilled, in a map, into the soothing conditions of a diagram. Every map is an abstraction of extreme eloquence: the externalized expression of a fundamental cognitive process that conceives of space and draws paths through it. Roads become lines. Cities become dots. States, provinces, countries become shapes. To use a map, you translate two dimensions back into three, transpose the lines and shapes onto roads and buildings. Google Street View is an odd inversion of this. It is as if the map grew curious about itself, flipped the abstraction inside out again. You're no longer on a line but in a street. The shapes that were lots are suddenly houses, storefronts, apartment buildings, parking lots, or shopping malls. The discretion embodied in the abstraction is gone, and its surface blooms into an almost garish specificity.

The defining feature of Google Street View is the access it offers to an unimaginable quantity of visual detail. Street signs and lawn furniture and plumbers' trucks and laundry lines. Shopping carts and construction dumpsters and strip malls and chain link fences with cardboard signs on them and electrical lines and fire hydrants and bus stop benches and trash bins and recycling bins and mailboxes and retaining walls and construction cones and bicycle racks. The illusion, however, is complicated. There's no one lens here but half a dozen or more. There's no shutter, only sensors. The camera moves, for the most part, atop an automobile, at a height of around eight feet. The correspondence is not, in other words, with the dimensions of the body, but with the scope of the inhuman future, where everything out there is out there to be seen, mapped, processed, analyzed, woven into machine logic. This inhuman eye moves as if through an inhuman climate, and you follow, advancing neither in steps nor even exactly on wheels but in short, linear thrusts, as if with rocket boosters. Click, swoosh; click, swoosh; click, swoosh.

All maps contain time to some degree, necessarily framing the moment in which they were made. These maps contain time strangely. In one click, down a single street, you pass from April 2012 to October 2018. In 2012, the road is wet with rain. In 2018, orange leaves carpet all the lawns and the trees are half bare. In Bishop, California, it's December 2007. Not only the season but the technology is different: The image is grainier. Light is rich and honey-like. In 2007, the financial crisis has not yet happened, Obama has not yet been elected president, and

I still live in California. Down another street, however, in July 2018, everything is crisp and bland. The financial crisis has come and gone; other crises loom.

From one click to the next, too, people disappear. It is sometimes impossible to find one's way back to them. This is so strange. Click, swoosh—turn around—click, swoosh. Gone. Their presence here is spectral. From the beginning, Google Street View raised privacy concerns. Men were seen leaving strip clubs—forever. These concerns, however, hinge on recognition, and attributions of value rooted in association. What of the massive, the really amazingly vast phenomenon of non-recognition and insignificance? Of these two facets, it is the latter that interests me, that I find the far more intriguing and profound. These walkers proceed from the nothing to the nowhere. Google Street View sees all but they are elusive, being no one, empty in regard to the system in which they exist, figments of something, a life, a name, a destination, you will never know.

Heidelberg

In the cabinet of a desk in a house in southern Colorado, I came across a packet of souvenir postcards from Heidelberg, Germany. There are nineteen cards in all, folded up like an accordion, depicting a selection of views and landmarks from around this evidently very old city, which straddles a river that weaves through a verdant valley, with low green hills on either side. The city—or so it appears in the postcards, for I've never been there—exists as a patchwork of historical epochs, one era piled atop the other. There is a red stone castle partly in ruin perched midway up the hillside to one side of the river. There are bridges at intervals crossing the river, including one with a massive, turreted gate, and river boats and ferries hauling tourists up and down. There are buildings with extravagant rococo facades and fine brick courtyards with statues in them. There's an interior corridor, perhaps in the castle, lined with antlers and tapestries and medieval statues. There's an enormous wine barrel packed into a cellar and a wood-paneled tavern with old wooden tables and a sign reading "Adolf Hitler Platz" hung up over an ancient radiator.

Judging from the pictures in which people appear, the packet itself likely dates to the early 1980s. The people wander these fine European courtyards with feathered hair, loose jeans and plastic shopping bags, an epoch in their own right layered over all the others, though they surely wouldn't have seen it that way, believing themselves—as we all do, in the moment—safely allied to the eternal present, fresh and modern amid all the old things. Forty years later, it is only too evident that they too are history, naïve and quaint, knowing nothing of the internet or melting glaciers.

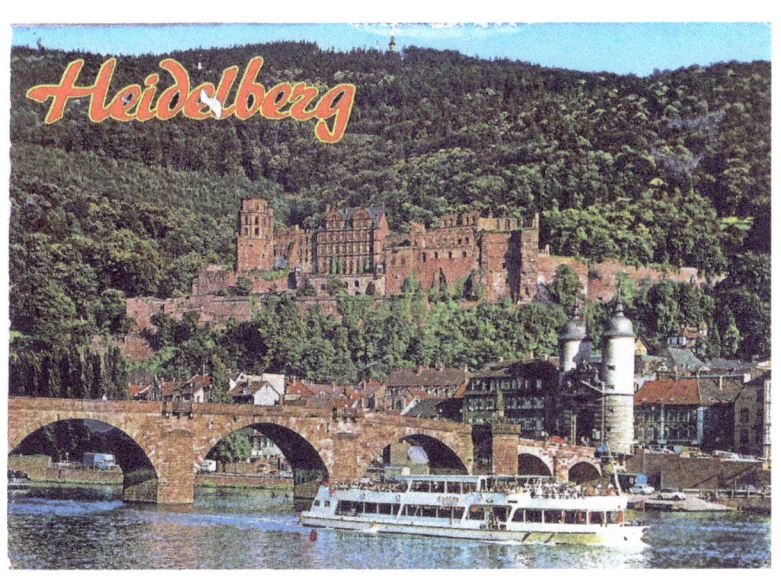

I've been to this house many times, over many years, and this packet of postcards has always been there. I don't know who left it—whether it was the person who actually went to Heidelberg or the person who received it from the person who did. I don't know if it belonged to the person whose house this once was or was left there later by someone else passing through.

The person whose house this once was—who built it, in fact—died more than thirty years ago. Most of the objects in the house were his and have remained more or less as he left them since his death: furniture, rugs, books, certain knick knacks, record albums and video cassettes; though as some things decay or fall apart or go missing, other things are added. No one else has lived in the house in all these years, though many, like myself, have passed through periodically, taking up residence for a night, a week, or a month or more, and those passing through sometimes leave things behind. This is to say that the contents of the house are a bit of a mix in regard to typically evident designations of being, such as whose and from where and to whom and for what.

It is generally easy to tell the difference between the objects that belonged to the man whose house this once was and the objects left by those passing through. The former have the feel of life lived on a daily basis by one with good taste and money to spend, while the latter have the feel of vacation time. In the kitchen, for example, there are first-hand dishes and second-hand dishes. The first-hand dishes were purchased as a set and with feeling, with real affection—they're a handsome modern design from Denmark that sells now on eBay for $150 a place setting; the second hand dishes are mismatched cast offs added to fill gaps and keep the kitchen operational. Similarly, there are good books and there are cheap books, which is to say: books that speak to the sustained cultivation of an intellectual life (Shakespeare, Dostoyevsky, Henry James, Harold Pinter), and books that speak to the passing of time while on holiday, at least for those to whom reading is not critical (Stephen King, Ann Rule, Frederick

Forsyth). There is a sense of permanence as well as identity to the objects belonging to the man whose house this was. It is possible, in staying there, to come to know this man. To the other objects there is a sense, primarily, of randomness and scrap, which has its own charm but is really an altogether different thing. A deck of cards here, a hiking map there, a mug from Lake Tahoe Summer of 1999. It is not possible to know anyone from crumbs like these; thus do the passers-through remain a mystery.

This packet of postcards, then, having identity in one sense but scrap in another, is difficult to place in either the story of the man who's house this once was or the faintly perceived flashes of energy that are the fleeting, passing stories of others. It is an anomaly, an orphan, without narrative. This is probably the reason I have loved it as I do.

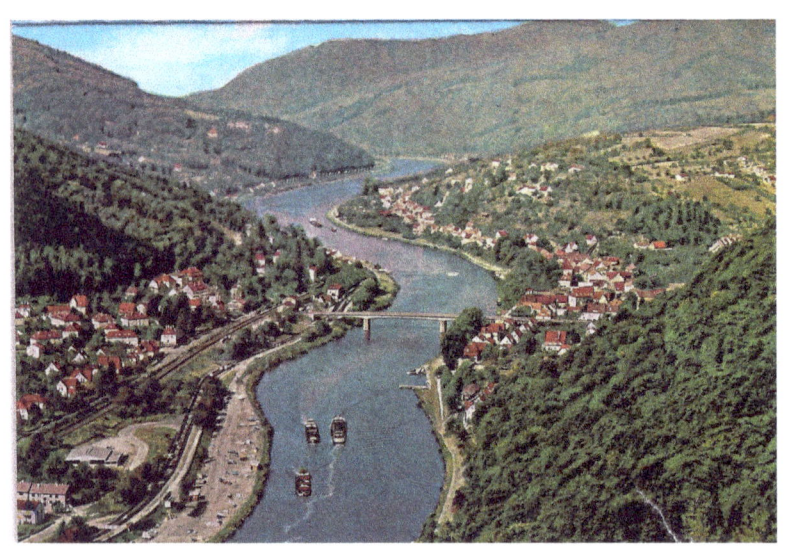

Next to the desk in which I found the packet of postcards from Heidelberg is a large, south-facing window. The window looks out on a bowl-shaped valley whose floor is carpeted with short, dry grasses that ripple through shades of tawny yellow, sienna and pale, chalky green, translucent across the pinkish earth, and chamisa whose fringe flares briefly every fall into an astonishing electric yellow before fading back to humble ochre. The valley is contained on all sides by the gentlest, pleasantest of hills, all wooded with juniper, scrub oak, piñon and pine. The sun bounds daily from left to right, invariably late to breach the hills to the east and early to sink below the ridge to the west. Clouds pass above at visible velocities. At night, stars gleam in a state of forgotten multitude, with no city lights to obscure them for hundreds of miles. From time to time, an exquisite white stillness settles across the valley and nothing moves anywhere while snow falls. Later, tracks of all kinds can be seen in the snow.

In the 1970s, hippies lived here in teepees scattered across the valley floor. Later, they built houses; some of these remain, others have collapsed into piles of rotting timber around disintegrating mattresses and shoes and ageless, interminable woodburning stoves. At some point, the hippies brought electricity in and dug a well at the lowest point on the property. They installed a system of pipes linking the well to a cistern up the hill to the west, where there is also a spring, and from there down again to each of the houses. Today, there are five habitable houses in the valley, three of which have permanent residents. Beyond this valley lies a scattering of modest ranches mostly, as well as summer homes for wealthy Texans tucked in among the aspens in the mountains to the west. There are only a few thousand people in the entire county, across a space of nearly 1,600 square miles.

There is history here, in this valley, of a human sort, but it's scant and thin and scarcely settles on the earth. It would not take much to blow it away. Where humans congregate in sufficient numbers, they grow heavy, build castles, endure. The valleys are laid with cobblestone streets and rooftops. Here, the congregation has been very slight and the earth continues magnificently and unperturbably to sound.

The man whose house this once was came from Denmark originally, from a wealthy family; his father was Danish, his mother American. He went to college in California, at Stanford. Then he joined a band and crossed the country in a bus. This man's young life, unlike my own, fell squarely into a historical moment of universally acknowledged iconic significance. In photographs from that time, he and his friends look so young and so quintessentially bohemian they might as well be out of a movie, with their handmade clothes and their bright, idealistic bodies.

This man's life, which I know partly by way of oral history and partly by way of a dot-matrix-printed memoir that lives on a shelf beside a lamp in the house, had numerous points of contact with the luminary aspects of the age. His band toured with Ken Kesey. He played once at a party along with Nina Simone. His close friend and bandmate, a woman named Trixie, appeared topless with her bass in Rolling Stone in 1969. He himself modelled for Robert Mapplethorpe. Sometime in the 1960s, he appeared on a program called The Joe Pyne Talk Show as a member of the audience keen to comment on the topic at hand, which was LSD. The footage, remarkably, can be found on YouTube. In the clip, which is one minute, forty-seven seconds long, he is so beautiful, so young, so smooth faced and precious you just want to cry to hear him talk.

Denmark shares a border with Germany—a small one, fifty kilometers wide at the base of the Jutland Peninsula. Heidelberg is 735 kilometers south of that border, a drive of just under eight hours. So it might have been he, the man whose house this once was, who acquired this packet of postcards himself, on holiday while visiting family or friends. In any case, he returned to Europe on numerous occasions, both while young, dressed up in his crazy clothes, and into his milder middle age.

What did he feel when he went back, after making of his life so perfect an American scene? Was he comforted or hampered by the narrow streets, the aged stone? I am inclined to believe it would have been a comfort to speak Danish round a table with Danes, over a meal unfolding in Danish time; to stroll the banks of wide rivers amid lush, green hills; to move through air in which history is suspended atmospherically—but that's me, who grew up in the American West, a descendent of Danes who fled poverty rather than wealth a century earlier, heir not to a castle legacy but a homestead one, and I am prone to rather fantastical notions of narrow streets and aged stone, as he must have been to notions of California.

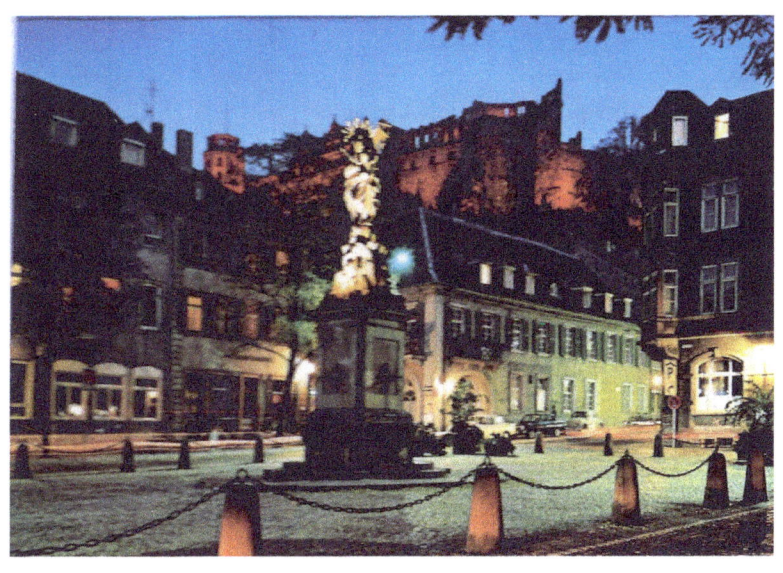

I came across a note in a journal from years ago, which I attribute there to William James, though I cannot locate its origin now:

"The great silence of the historical vacuum."

He was speaking of Stanford, California, where he spent a semester teaching in 1906. But the words capture (and this is surely why I wrote them down) a certain sensation associated with landscape across much of the American West, and far more so today this quiet stretch of Colorado than the place we now call Silicon Valley. The words aren't true, exactly: there is history here, as I said before, just not enough of it to quite accumulate physically; or rather, not enough of quite the right type. It is a passing-through history, not a building-up one. A history of claiming, extracting, massacring, yes, but not of erecting castles and defending them. It is a history of transitory ownership, of (in more or less reverse order) Texan summer houses, hippies, ranchers, highways, coal miners, railroads, homesteaders, cowboys, shepherds, the Santa Fe trail, Mexican settlers, traders, American explorers, Spanish explorers, Comanche, Ute and Jicarilla Apache. Like the grasses across the valley floor, any visible imprint is stretched very thin, which does leave a silence, and the perception of a vacuum.

But there is no shaking history off. Visible or invisible, it is a membrane that binds us all as human, to one another and to the land. The hippies, coming here, thought they'd found something empty that they could fill, a place to build a new kind of life. What's striking, though, in their pictures and stories, is how steeped it all was in historical nostalgia: in the narrative of the American pioneer, as well as romanticized notions of Native American life. No one breaks with history; it isn't possible.

What's striking, also, in this perception of vacuity, is a certain willful, almost desperate blindness. The explorers, coming here, thought they'd found something empty that they could fill. But they could believe this only by refusing to look, or else by decimating all that they saw.

It is true, however, that in comparison to Heidelberg, on Heidelberg's terms, this little valley is very silent indeed. On a hill overlooking the city of Heidelberg are the ruins of a Celtic fortress dating to the fifth century BC. A Roman fort was installed there five hundred years later and the Romans remained until 260 AD, when they were driven out by Germanic tribes. The village that preceded Heidelberg, called Bergheim, first appears in the historical record in 769 AD. Several monasteries and abbeys followed, and the first reference to Heidelberg itself appears in one of those abbeys, in a document dating to 1196. The university was founded in 1386. Every era a new layer—of masonry, of documents, of tools, of ideology, of style, of raw human energy: ambition and suffering.

This silence, we in America call freedom, and we in the American West only more so. If freedom from history is not actually possible, it is freedom, at least, from historical density, which, by virtue of its own intrinsic inertia, seeks to define the future on the basis of the past.

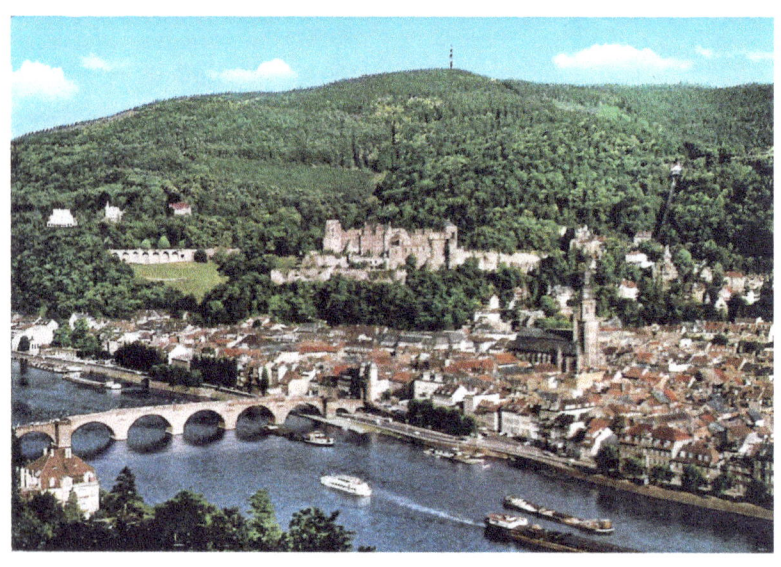

One Heidelberg landmark not pictured among the postcards is the Thingstätte amphitheater, which was built by the Nazi party on the very hill where the Celtic fortress and the Roman encampment once stood. The hill is called Heiligenberg, or Holy Mountain—a designation made much of by Joseph Goebbels, Hitler's Minister of Propaganda, who received his PhD from Heidelberg University in 1921, in his address at the opening of the amphitheater on June 22, 1935. The site was chosen for its supposedly Germanic past. According to one writer on the website Failed Architecture:

> The amphitheater was said to be located where the Germans gathered themselves: some archaeological research was done very hastily in order to testify to the 'sacred' value of the area even if no evidence of the presence of Germanic people was to be found. The memory, as well as the history of the city, was thereby manipulated, and the legitimation of the construction was to be found at the heart of this very same manipulation since the archaeological research wasn't actually scientific.[1]

The opening of the Thingstätte amphitheater drew 20,000 people. The Nazis intended to build 400 of these amphitheaters across the Reich for the production of a new, multidisciplinary form of drama that, in the words of one of Goebbels' underlings, "intensifies historical events to create a mythical, universal, unambiguous reality beyond reality." They only managed twelve, however, and the fad died out within a couple of years.

The amphitheater—now somewhat mossy and overgrown—looks like an egg, like a spaceship, like a Greek temple, like a vulva, like a sacrificial platform in a B-grade Bible movie, like a ziggurat, like a sports arena; above all, like a fascist monument, which is to say like a blunt expression of power drawing lustily on the power contained in the architecture of other eras. It's been a state-protected site since the late 1980s, but nothing much has ever been done with it, save the installation of a couple of plaques. Primarily, it seems, it's been known as a party spot, at least until a fire broke out in 2017 and the unsanctioned annual festivity known as Walpurgis Night was shut down. An apparently outdated Wikipedia page says of the site today: "Thousands of mostly young people congregate there to drum, to breathe fire, and to juggle."[2]

There is a dirt road that weaves between the hills to the south up through a grove of aspens to a gate where another property begins; it is a good place for walking and listening to books and the last time I was there, I listened to a book about Martin Luther. Luther was born in the town of Eisleben, in central Germany, in 1483, and spent much of his life in the town of Wittenberg, roughly eighty kilometers to the east. I was struck, in the book, by all Luther's walking. From the moment he published his Ninety-five Theses disputing the sale of indulgences by the Roman Catholic Church in 1517 through to his excommunication in 1521, he was continually traversing the roads of medieval Germany to defend himself in one ecclesiastical court or another—on foot, generally, in a friar's sandals and robes. They were roads, I imagine, not so different from this one: hard-packed and rutted in dry weather, boggy and slick and tiresome in wet weather; still and solitary most of the time, with the wild sky above and the company of trees and a thousand small, half-invisible birds; though beleaguered with threats I can only imagine: bandits and thieves, news of the plague, religious zealots engaged in campaigns of terror.

In April of 1518, Luther traveled to Heidelberg—400 kilometers south of Wittenberg—to deliver what is known as the Heidelberg Disputation. The university in Heidelberg was 132 years old by that time. There were monasteries several hundred years older. There is a plaque now in one of the fine brick courtyards marking the site where the disputation was given, installed on the five hundredth anniversary of Luther's birth, right around the time I estimate the packet of postcards from Heidelberg was made. The disputation was Luther's first opportunity to publicly declare and defend his evolving theology since the publication of the Ninety-five Theses, and as he was asked by his host to avoid the controversial bits (indulgences, purgatory, the Pope, etc.), he spoke instead—and this is an important first—on the chasm, as he saw it, between grace and good works. He declared to his fellow Augustinians in Heidelberg: "The law says, 'do this,' and it is never done. Grace says, 'believe in this,' and everything is already done."³

I find it pleasing to be walking this road in Colorado while simultaneously walking, with Luther, this road to Heidelberg, over a distance of more than five hundred years. I am here and I am there, where I've never been and couldn't be, simultaneously. His was a big life that changed the whole world, mine is a small one that will change very little, but we are alike in this: two legs, two feet, a torso and a brain, going down a quiet, rutted dirt road. History, of course, will have nothing to do with walking, nothing to do with roads like these, unless they play in to some special drama—such as when Luther walked through a lightning storm and swore to God he'd be a monk if he made it out alive.

But think of what these walks entailed: Every step he took toward one or another disputation over the course of these four years, anticipating what he would say, and every step he took heading home after, mulling over what he did in fact say, was a step in which he wrestled with himself and what he was up against and the prospect of his own very likely demise. Did he believe that what he said—condemning exploitation, superstition, hypocrisy, greed, an appalling system of institutional corruption—was true? Did he believe it enough to be killed for having said it, and killed in some truly awful way, burned or skinned or torn apart limb by limb in several directions? He had miles and miles, kilometers and kilometers, to come again and again to the same answer: Yes. Later in his life, when he was no longer obliged to walk long distances in sandals, he came to many far worse conclusions, such as that Jews were a "base, whoring people" whose homes and schools and temples should be burned, and that peasants standing up for their rights should be slaughtered. It is easier, surely, to go mad in this way while shut up inside among those who admire you than it is out on the road face to face with your god.

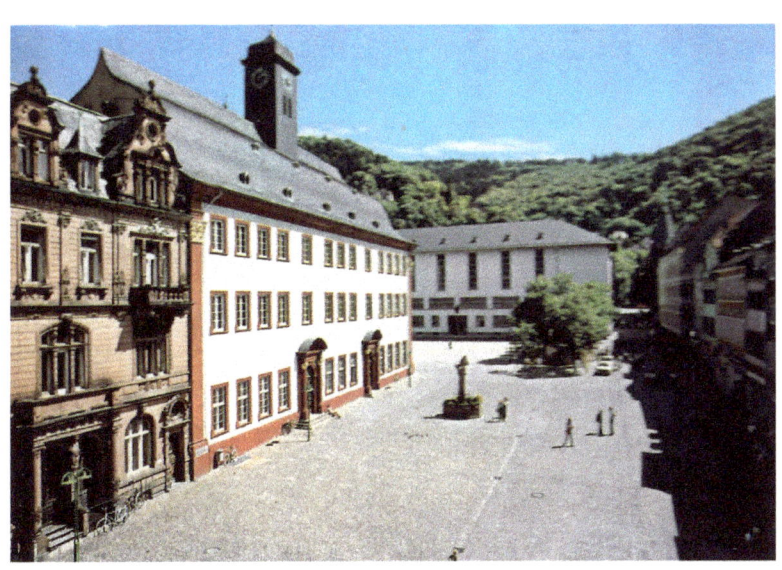

One day, upon arriving at this house, I found the packet of postcards in a trash bin beside the desk. This was disconcerting. Had it fallen there by accident? Or had someone intended to throw it away? Both seemed improbable. How could it fall by accident when the desk was closed? But if someone meant to throw it away—well, first of all: Why? And second, why not actually throw it then—i.e., why not actually take out the trash? It was the only thing left in that or any other trash bin, as the house had been cleaned since the prior lodger.

The thought of someone willfully discarding this object distressed me, in part because it is so precious an object and in part because it raised a difficult question: If this of all objects can end up in the trash, one of the desk's most precious secrets, what else might these heedless strangers discard? This house, clearly, is not mine; I have no say over what comes and goes. But still I want it to stay always and forever as it is.

At the same time, finding the packet of postcards in the trash bin presented an opportunity, gave me license—by one interpretation, anyway—that I had probably wanted all along to claim it, and I did. I took it home. It pleased me to have it because then I could look anytime I liked. Also, then I knew it was safe.

But I feel ashamed of taking it. The fact remains that it wasn't mine to take. I could have asked, couldn't I? It is entirely likely that no one would have cared, that no one even recalled it was there. But I didn't ask. It's true that I've brought many objects into this house over the years. A cheap red kettle whose interior coating soon chipped off. Later, an electric kettle of higher quality. Several pots and pans. A toaster oven. A set of four crystal wine glasses I found in a thrift store that made a beautiful ringing sound when struck, three of which have now disappeared. An abridged copy of Somerset Maugham's *Of Human Bondage* that I bought in a library sale in a nearby town and only later noticed was abridged (and thus junk). Margaret Drabble's *The Needle's Eye*. Ivy Compton-Burnett's *Pastors and Masters*. Russell Banks' *Rule of the Bone*. A copy of one of my own books, which subsequently disappeared. One can say I've given far more than I've taken, at least as far as objects go, but that is clearly not the way morality works.

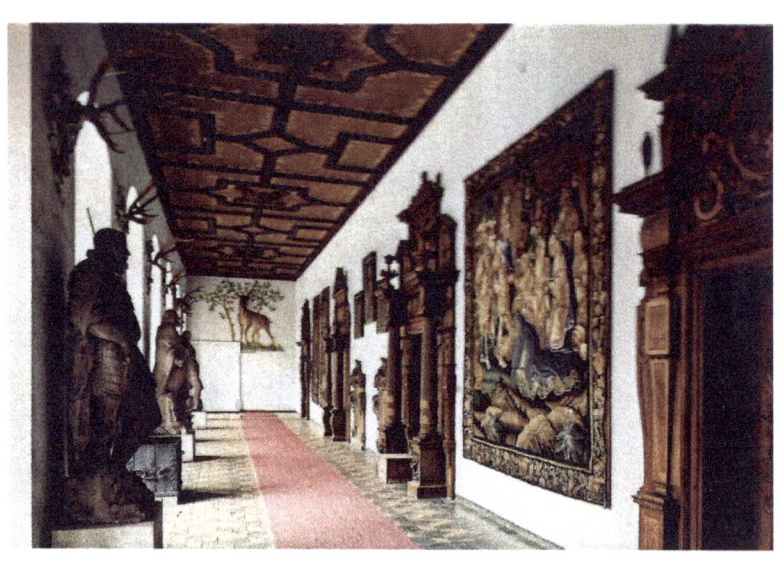

Ownership is an interesting issue in this place, meaning this house as well as the valley as a whole. The property that encompasses this valley is technically owned by a cattle corporation, though the shares belong to hippies, not ranchers—including those who pitched in to buy the land initially as well as those who've lived on it for some period of time. This particular ownership structure was adopted by the founders when the property was purchased because the other congregation of hippies in the area, across the larger valley beyond the hills to the east, purchased their land as a nonprofit organization and were later resented by neighbors for not paying taxes. The founders here wanted to not make the same mistake. The shareholders, so far as I can gather, are mostly in their later years (or deceased), and distributed far and wide across the earth. There are five remaining who live here year-round, two couples and one individual. Legally, I suppose, the houses they built belong to them personally.

To whom does the house that was built by the man who died belong? Technically (or so I once heard), it was willed to the son of the couple who live nearest the house, just about shouting distance across the valley to the south. This son, who would have been fairly young at that time, is now grown, though not in a position to either live in or care for the house, as he does not live independently himself but with a state-appointed caretaker in a city several hundred miles away. It is the couple, his parents, who tend to the house, rout out its mice and pay its taxes; in a legal sense, then, as well as a practical one, it certainly belongs to them.

It is still referred to, however, as this man's house, in this man's name. Energetically, it still belongs to him, which may be to say it belongs to his memory, though what one feels, in the house, is thicker and more palpable than personal memory. In any case, I have no memory of this man, for I never met him. Yet I feel this thing, this presence that persists in retaining ownership, quite distinctly throughout the house and its environs. It has something to do with the ubiquity of this man's possessions; something to do with his involvement in the design and construction of the house (along with the man from the house across the valley to the south); something to do with a notion that no one has yet let drop—the notion of a life that remains in existence so long as there is someone to think it.

Love too, though, confers a degree of ownership—in any case, it wants to. It tries to. Love is, to some degree, possessive by nature, even a love as liberal as I know mine to be. I have no legal, no financial, no familial claim to this house, nor to the valley in which it resides; I have no particular emotional connection to the utopian vision that was its genesis. But I love the house and the valley intensely.

I love the shape of the house, its comfortable layout. I love its windows and its views. I love its little fold out desk, and the simple stool that is the desk's only chair. I love its stylish Danish tableware. I love its generosity of spirit, its embrace of all who pass through its doors, whether friend or stranger, and its quiet endurance despite them all. I love its smell. I love its wood plank floors and claw foot tub. I love its interminable wood burning stove. I love its isolation, which is also to say I love what it lacks: internet access, cell service, a telephone line, television, even radio—any avenue of connectivity outside of electricity, running water, and friendship. Above all, I love its silence, which is like silence nowhere else I know, a connoisseur's silence, rich and thick and undisturbed by the toxic, unrelenting buzz of our age.

I love the dry, hard soil across the valley floor. I love the shape of the hills. I love the shape of the frame the hills make around the sky. I love the clouds with their ever changing life up there. I love the first morning light on the peak to the west, and the last glowing gold across the treetops to the east. I love the woodpeckers, jays, and chickadees. I love the chipmunks who dash with marvelous agility across the rocks, gathering, distributing, surveying, frolicking, as well as the bobcats, bears and mountain lions who so rarely allow themselves to be seen. I love the pale, dry grasses. I love the aspens up the hard, rutted road that leads through the hills to a gate where another property begins. I've walked up and down that road so many times, at so many hours and in so many seasons, in sun, snow, wind, rain, mud, in so many moods, having so many thoughts, and every time I love it anew.

My love gathers the whole place up for myself and feels entitled to what it finds, proclaiming in the closest, least audible of whispers: "Mine." I know it isn't, and don't believe it should be. If it was actually mine, some part of it would die. I would install conveniences. I would bring in too many of my own possessions. So my stake is a very private stake, an imaginative stake or more poetically, a spiritual one, valid in the clerk's office of my own history solely, which is no small thing, so far as I am concerned. What legal ownership does grant, however, that spiritual ownership doesn't—what it grants indeed above all, as its first principal—is continuity, and certainly I fear the day I will lose access to this house. What will become of the land when all the shareholders are gone is as yet, far as I know, undetermined, for settling the question involves lawyers, and coordination between far flung interests, and above all money that the shareholders don't have. Someday, though, inevitably, something will be decided which will in all likelihood exclude from its rationale bonds of love, friendship, loyalty, and care—thus will I be cast out of this place.

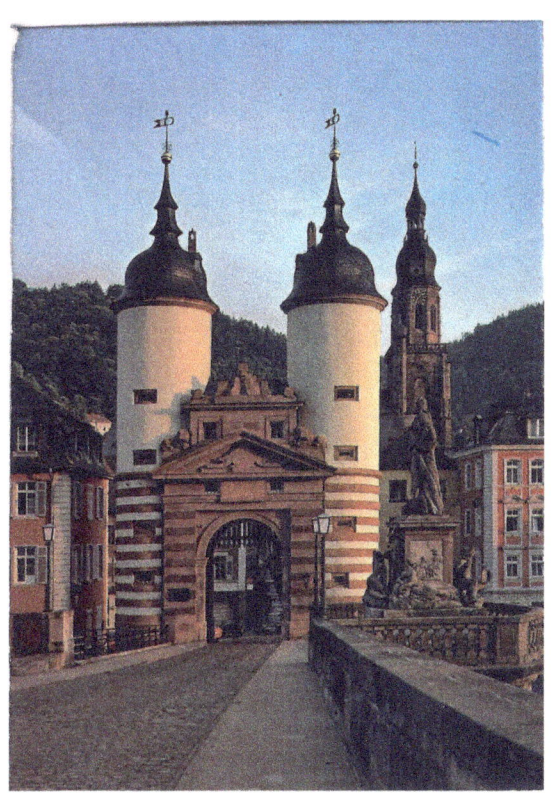

The young people saunter, in Heidelberg, as if they own the place. History means very little to the young. It is as if a certain accumulation of time in the body is necessary to fathom the accumulation of time in the world. Note on the far left side of the picture, however: two elderly ladies in knee-length skirts with purses. In the context of the picture, they contain time differently, closer to the way the buildings do. The very structure of their clothing is history. And think of what the span of their time on this earth has contained!—a rupture like no other to the fabric of humanity.

Where were they in 1933, when the National Socialist German Workers' Party secured nearly half the popular vote in Heidelberg? Or two weeks later, when Hitler passed the Enabling Act, transforming his government into a dictatorship? In 1938, when Nazi rioters burned 267 synagogues across Germany and Austria in a single night, including two synagogues in Heidelberg? In March of 1945, when the Nazis fled, destroying three arches of the historic bridge as they went, and, one day later, the U.S. Army marched in? In the twelve years between the Nazis' rise to power and their fall at the end of World War II, half of the faculty of Heidelberg University was fired for racial or political reasons, and 800 Jews—out of a population of 1,100—were killed, deported or fled. Where were these ladies on each of those terrible days?

The philosopher Karl Jaspers, who was forced to resign his post at Heidelberg University in 1937 and was among the first to return in 1945, said upon returning, in a speech delivered at the reopening of the university: "When our Jewish friends were led away, we did not go out into the streets, we did not shout until we too were liquidated. No, we preferred to stay alive, with the feeble though correct thought that our death would not have been of any issue anyhow. It remains our guilt that we are still alive."[4] Did the ladies with the purses feel the same? Or did they feel some other way, as they stood there chatting in the castle courtyard?

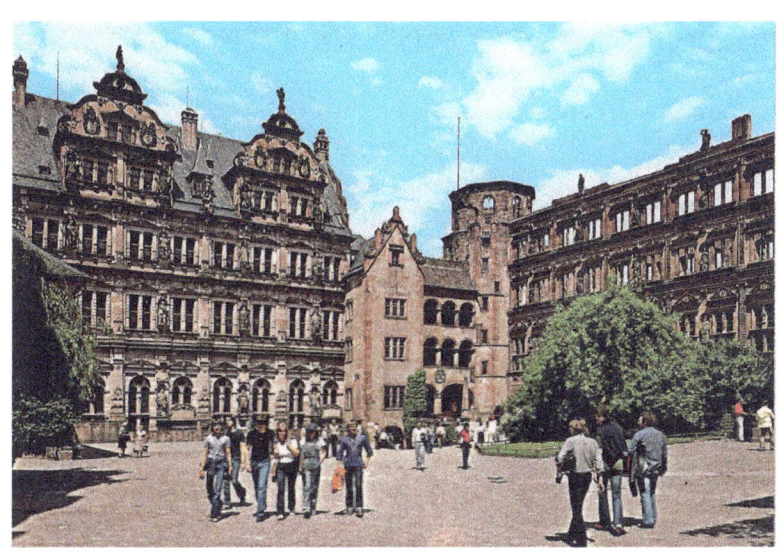

There is a ruin very high up the hill to the west of the valley, just below the windy ridge: a one-room cabin with a little loft, the roof caving in, the windows blown out. What a view! the hippies must have thought up there—and indeed it is, just stunning, you can see all across the valley and miles beyond to the mountains that trace the eastern horizon. They only lasted a summer, however.

For one thing, there's no road up there. It's difficult to get to, even on foot. Somehow, despite this, they hauled cement for the foundation, loads of logs and lumber, shingles, tar paper and mortar, a woodburning stove, a gas range, windows, a couch, carpets, and scores of beer and soda cans. It's all still there, all this stuff, crumbling and rotting before this beautiful view. A plastic doll lies naked, bleached by the sun, on the floorboards, surrounded by shards of broken glass, like a maudlin allusion to human futility and fate in a bad experimental film.

There are several such ruins around the valley, each with its own no longer knowable story, but this one may be the most impressive for its brazen and poetic folly. It must have been one glorious summer, waking up every morning to such a view, in a cabin whose every hand-laid log was testament to that very American dream of finding some new and better way to live. Turns out, however, that roads are useful. Running water is useful. Electricity is useful. The houses that lasted out here all have those things.

What's most striking, today, about all these ruins is how abruptly and completely they were abandoned. They belonged, these builders, to an idealistic generation, yet when the ideal proved untenable, it was—by many, at least—simply dropped. No demolition, no disposal, no recycling or re-use. The houses were just *left* there—all that work, all that hope, all that stuff. It's the stuff that's particularly shocking now, at least from the vantage of my own decidedly less idealistic generation. What did they think would become of it all? The plastic dolls, the boots, the soda cans, the magazines, the mattresses, the coffee cups, the flower jars, the hand-painted doors and now-broken windows. It's junk, and not all of it biodegradable junk. Maybe they thought it would all just dissolve, but decades have passed and it's all still there. Really dissolving would take a century or more, and even then the woodburning stoves will remain, and microscopic flakes of plastic and chemical paint.

What did they think, that this land was just theirs to clutter up and abandon? That it was empty when they came, devoid of history, and empty would remain once they left? The hubris of the American West is blindness; the blindness is a kind of disease.

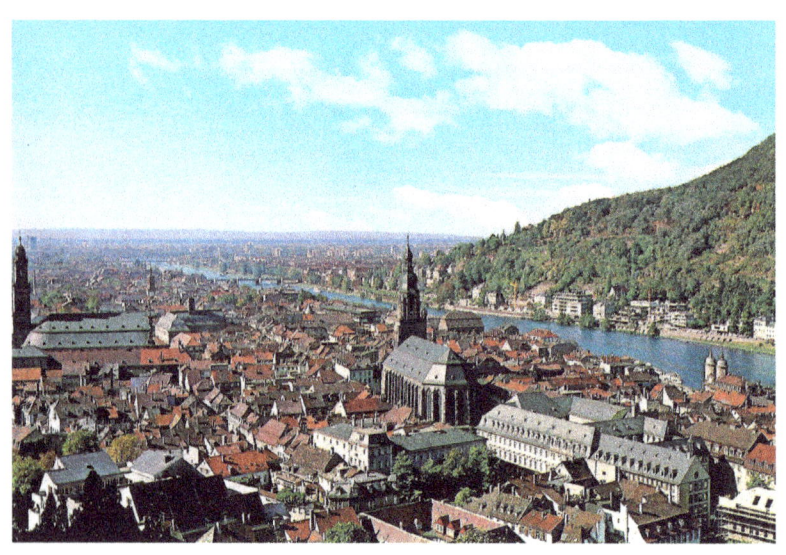

It is strange to think of William James in California, on the very grounds, in the very classrooms perhaps, where the man whose house this once was came himself to study, from Denmark. James was awake in his bed early on the morning of April 18, 1906, when the Great San Francisco Earthquake hit. Lasting roughly sixty seconds, the earthquake was felt from southern Oregon to Los Angeles and inland as far as central Nevada; along with the fires it ignited, it killed an estimated 3,000 people and destroyed nearly 500 city blocks, leaving 400,000 residents homeless.

James's experience on that morning is recorded with characteristic observational enthusiasm in an essay titled "On Some Mental Effects of the Earthquake":[5]

> The emotion consisted almost wholly of glee and admiration; glee at the vividness which such an abstract idea or verbal term as 'earthquake' could put on when translated into sensible reality and verified concretely; and admiration at the way in which the frail little wooden house could hold itself together in spite of such a shaking. I felt no trace whatever of fear; it was pure delight and welcome.

In his own reactions as well as the reactions of those he speaks to in the aftermath, James is struck by a certain dislocation of interpretation—in particular, a lack of fear. Also by an inclination to personify. ("Animus and intent were never more present in any human action," he writes of the quake.) Even in San Francisco itself, which he visited several times in subsequent days, the reactions he observes are peculiarly out of alignment with the reality at hand: industriousness, cheerfulness, equanimity in the face of devastation, death, and ruin. For James, it attests to two enduring human tendencies: to make order out of chaos, and to make the best of what must be got through. He writes:

Surely the cutting edge of all our usual misfortunes comes from their character of loneliness. We lose our health, our wife or children die, our house burns down, or our money is made way with, and the world goes on rejoicing, leaving us on one side and counting us out from all its business. In California everyone, to some degree, was suffering, and one's private miseries were merged in the vast general sum of privation and in the all-absorbing practical problem of general recuperation. The cheerfulness, or, at any rate, the steadfastness of tone, was universal. Not a single whine or plaintive word did I hear from the hundred losers whom I spoke to. Instead of that there was a temper of helpfulness beyond the counting.

The uniquely American aspect of this reaction to trauma is not lost on James—"In an exhausted country, with no marginal resources," he admits, "the outlook on the future would be much darker"—but it's clear in reading the essay today, in the wake of so many subsequent traumas (World War I, World War II, the Holocaust, Hiroshima, the Vietnam War, the HIV/AIDS epidemic, the wars in Iraq, Afghanistan and Syria, the climate crisis), how prettily James's America was sitting just then. In San Francisco in 1906, it would indeed have been possible to think: We'll just rebuild! In Heidelberg in 1945, the outlook was a whole different register of complicated.

And now? Today? As fires consume larger and larger swaths of both California and Colorado every year and the pond in this little valley sits dry for the first time since the hippies drilled their well, the steadfastness of tone is not quite so universal.

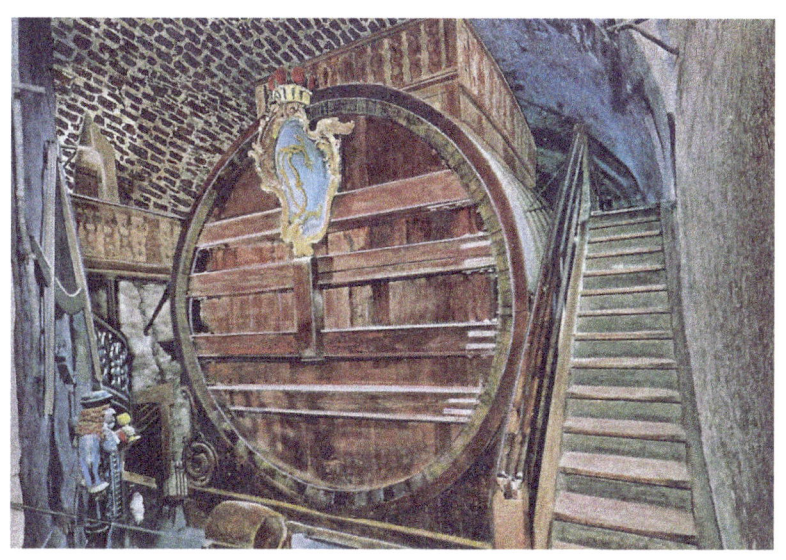

Memory is like masonry: it can be built up or blown out. It can be built up around a blown out part, or, once built on a seemingly solid foundation, can sag and tilt slowly over the years into a blown out part that's been ignored or untended. Heidelberg was unusual in World War II in that it was never bombed; architecturally, then, it remained in 1945 more or less as it had been in 1933, which was much as it had been for centuries. It was, almost alone among German cities, unscarred.

But only, of course, architecturally. In a series of lectures Karl Jaspers delivered in Heidelberg in 1945, titled "The Question of German Guilt," the war and preceding Nazi occupation reverberate palpably through every word like ringing in the ears from an explosion. Here we see a man picking through not the physical but the social and intellectual rubble in the attempt to restore a university—and by extension, a nation—locked for twelve years in the grip of totalitarian propaganda and terror. "We must restore the readiness to think," he says, "against the tendency to have everything prepared in advance and, as it were, placarded in slogans."[6]

Part of this relearning to think was relearning how to behave as a thinker in public, without masks, without fear, also without pride or defiance or revenge or scorn. ("All through these years we have heard other people scorned. We do not want to continue that.") Also how to participate democratically, how to respect difference, how to disagree peacefully. Conversation remained a minefield. To hold one's tongue in the world but rage in private, he says, is to evade reality and corrode the self. The opposite, however, is no better.

> Talking with each other is canceled too by speech which no longer speaks in private—speech which means to insult but not to hear an answer, waiting rather for the moment of face-slapping and secretly anticipates what in reality is fist and manslaughter, machine gun and bombing plane. Rage can

distinguish only friend and foe for a life-and-death struggle, talks frankly with neither and does not see men as men, to get along with by being ready for self-corrections. We cannot be conscientious enough in illuminating this sort of conflict and rupture in our intercourse.

I know that comparisons are dangerous things, especially where Nazi Germany is concerned, but I am moved, in reading these words, by their applicability to our own divided and angry America, where "speech which means to insult but not to hear an answer" is all we seem to ever hear.

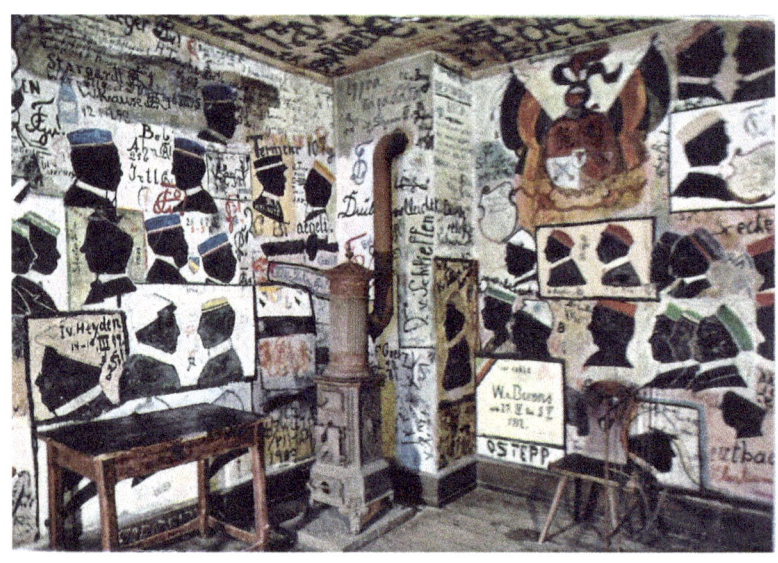

History and power are uniquely allied. All regimes write their own history; totalitarian regimes do so nearly from scratch, phantasmagorically, as Hannah Arendt illustrates in her great book *The Origins of Totalitarianism*. Whole new worlds of the past unfurl within their bubble of power, in support of their power, to position and enable it.

In Germany, Arendt argues, the "monstrous forgeries in historiography of which all totalitarian regimes are guilty" found unlikely sympathy within another, co-existing bubble of power, the intellectual elite, who enjoyed the privilege of having no faith in history, who felt they knew enough to see through the whole game and thus "did not object at all to paying a price, the destruction of civilization, for the fun of seeing how those who had been excluded unjustly in the past forced their way into it."[7] Her contempt for this particular class of thinker is scathing.

> To this aversion of the intellectual elite for official historiography, to its conviction that history, which was a forgery anyway, might as well be the playground of crackpots, must be added the terrible, demoralizing fascination in the possibility that gigantic lies and monstrous falsehoods can eventually be established as unquestioned facts, that man may be free to change his own past at will, and that the difference between truth and falsehood may cease to be objective and become a mere matter of power and cleverness, of pressure and infinite repetition.

Arendt, a student and later friend of Karl Jaspers, also received her PhD from Heidelberg University, eight years after Joseph Goebbels. Arendt fled Germany in 1933, after being imprisoned for a time with her mother by the Gestapo. Joseph Goebbels, when his bubble of power, his enabling, phantasmagorical history collapsed, killed his six young children, his wife, and himself in a bunker in Berlin.

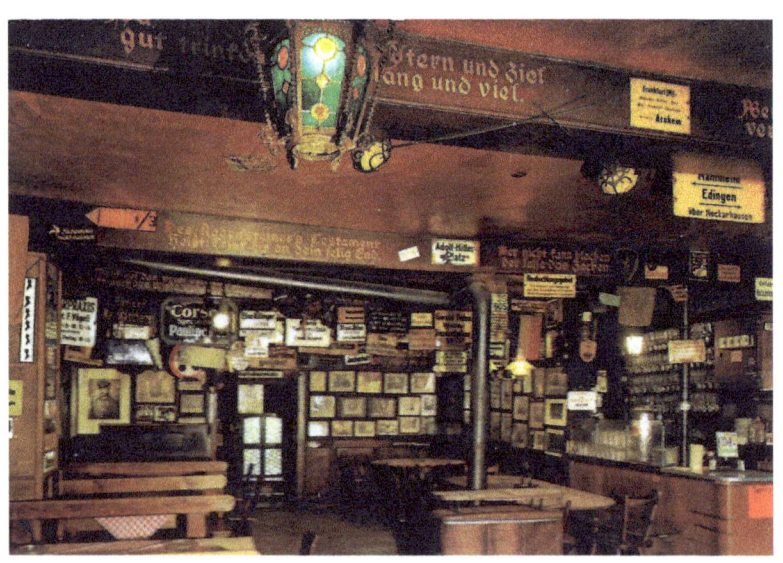

In the clip on YouTube from The Joe Pyne Talk Show, the man whose house this once was wears a flouncy print blouse suggestive of the nineteenth century. He was very handsome, like a movie actor. It's his voice, however, that comes as a shock after knowing him only through photographs and stories: it's soft and earnest, slightly theatrical, intelligent.

This fellow Joe Pyne asks him what he has to say and he turns the tables, says that as the topic at hand is LSD, and as he's taken LSD himself (he is in fact on LSD at this moment, though he says so only later, in his memoir), maybe this fellow Joe Pyne has questions for him. Joe Pyne does; his questions are like jabs from a thick, heavy club given that he really has no interest in the answers.

> Joe Pyne: Why do you take it?
> Him: Why do I take it? Because I learn a great deal from taking it.
> Joe Pyne: What have you learned from it?
> Him: I've learned what, to me, life is about and what maybe I can do—
> Joe Pyne: By the way, I've heard this phrase so much tonight I'm going to pursue it. What is life really like?
> Him: To me?
> Joe Pyne: You say you've learned what life is really like. That's a [indecipherable] statement. Now please tell me what you've learned.
> Him: I've learned to be totally aware of what's going on with myself and with the people around me.
> Joe Pyne: I asked you a question: What is life really like? You say—
> Him: [Here he begins to push back; his voice rises slightly.] To me, life is total awareness!
> Joe Pyne: Well, what does that mean? Aren't you totally aware that you're standing here, you're on television—

> Him: And every game you're playing with me I'm totally aware of too. Every game you're playing with Dr.— [He points to the other guest on the show; his name is unclear.]
> Joe Pyne: What game? I'm looking for information! How are you more aware under the drug than you are right this minute?
> Him: I'm not saying under—I didn't say I was *under* the drug more aware of what's going on but I'm certainly not coming on as a national authority writing those trite books like that either. [Laughter from the audience. This is referring to a book by Dr. Whomever.]
> Joe Pyne: Have you read it?
> Him: Yeah, I have, word for word.
> Joe Pyne: And you think it's trite?
> Him: Very.
> Joe Pyne, turning to the camera: We'll be back after this word from the sponsor playing *his* game.

Joe Pyne says this last bit with an arch of one eyebrow—a smug, middle aged white man in a suit, at a desk alongside another slightly older smug white man in a suit. Wikipedia says of this fellow, Joe Pyne: "He ridiculed hippies (a favorite target), homosexuals, and feminists"—all of which this beautiful young man was. But in this case, the young man doesn't come off the worst for it, knowing perhaps, in his marvelous LSD trance, that he was the one on the right side of history, or at least the side more ardently mythologized.

Within a few years of this exchange, Joe Pyne would be dead from lung cancer at 45. Twenty years after that, at around the same age, this young man would also be dead, from AIDS. What are these traces that remain, that we patch together into the shape of a life, even in the absence of personal memory? They do persist, these fragments; they are tangible and real. A bit of black and white film stock, digitized and posted for who knows what reason by who knows whom on the internet: one minute, forty-seven seconds in the lives of these two individuals who had little in common and no fellow feeling, who were playing out roles on opposite sides of the great American drama of their day. It's a souvenir now, this clip, but of time instead of place. But a souvenir has nothing to say to the death bed, does it?

The man whose house this once was did not die in this house. At some point over the course of his illness—perhaps when he knew he would not get better—he travelled back to California, to die in a house belonging to two close friends from the hippie days, in San Diego. I've been to that house too; it is a lovely place settled into over several decades now, with children grown up and gone away, full of photo albums and old film footage transferred to digital video, for example of the bus that toured the band around with Ken Kesey parked in a field in Connecticut on the occasion of this couple's barefoot wedding. The house is really a small compound: house and guest house and art studio, all arranged in the back around a lush California courtyard. It would have been a pleasant, a peaceful place to die, I imagine, if any place is, though so different from this valley here, with its absence of courtyards, with its dry soil, its rawness, its clear, bright air.

It was in the guest house in the back where the man lay as he died. There is an addendum to the dot-matrix-printed memoir, written by these friends, recounting the last few days of the man's life. It's painful to read. One of the two writes, near the end: "For those last few hours, I felt that he was gone. He was not seeing, though his eyes were open. He looked as if he had stepped away from a non-working body."

Did the house here, in Colorado, shudder and quiver at just that moment, as some essential part of its own soul went out? I am inclined to think so. Yet it held, it did not crumble: empty, solid. And winter after winter, it remains. The last time I was there, the wind blew like crazy through the November night, night after night, with a ferocity that seemed to have personality in it, "animus and intent," specifically of a female and adolescent nature. In moments, I thought it (she) would tear the roof off the frame. She didn't, of course. The house persists, through decades, with quiet dignity.

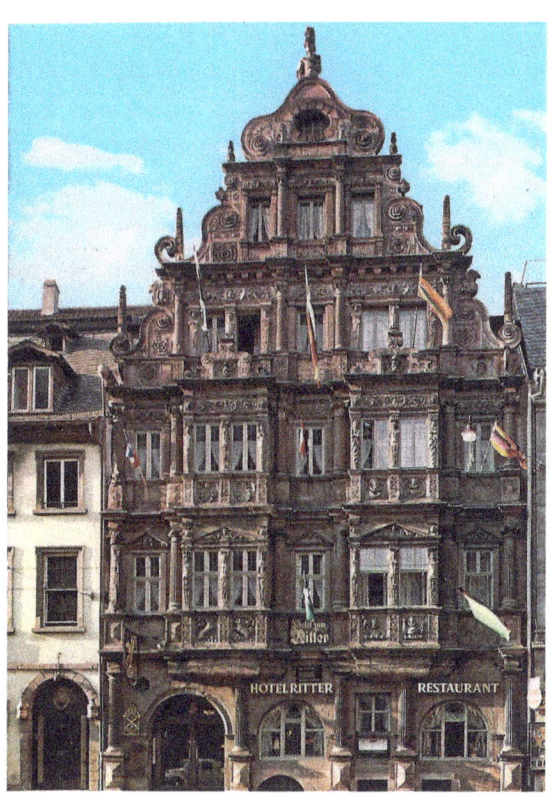

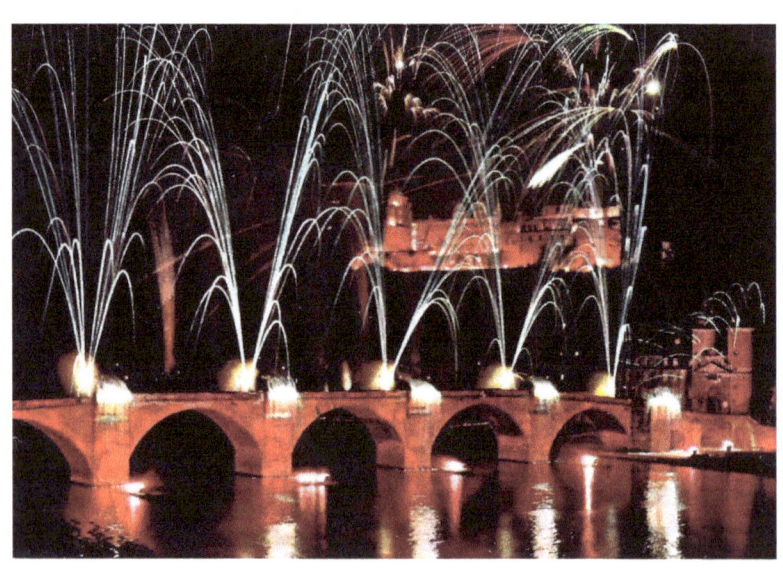

An earthquake is like an earthquake. A war is like an earthquake. A revolution is like an earthquake (political or sexual). A death is like an earthquake. AIDS was like an earthquake.

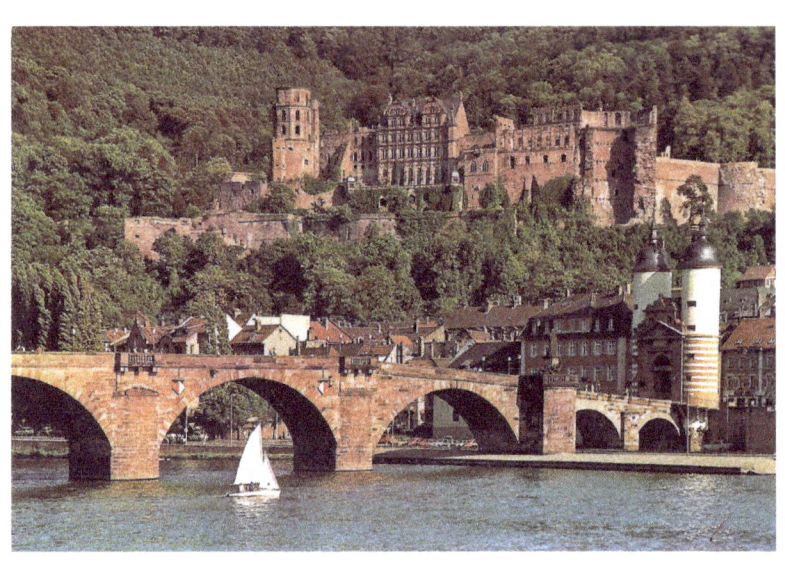

The decomposition of a house—this outer shell, this second body—is quite different from the decomposition of a body. The body will go whether you like it or not, eventually. The house will go when the body leaves it and the mice move in and shred all the cushions. If passed on to others, however, and properly tended, a house can last for centuries. Tending, for a house, requires love, and this house has that; also money, which it has less of, but manages.

A castle is a different matter. The decomposition of a house requires abandonment, forgetting, but castles, which are, in one sense, just very big houses, are not especially easy to forget. Indeed, the entire point of a castle is to impose remembering—of itself, its inhabitants, certain structures of power—on all who behold it. They are rarely just abandoned. They are often, however, besieged, conquered, and physically battered, all of which can lead to ruin. It was certainly the case with Heidelberg Castle.

The castle was built sometime prior to 1214. It grew into two adjacent castles over the course of the next hundred years, but one of the two was destroyed by lightning in 1537. The remaining castle was captured by Spanish-Imperial forces in 1622, in the Thirty Years' War. It was captured by the Swedes, for some reason, in 1633. It changed hands a few more times after that before being set fire to by the French, along with much of the town, in the Nine Years War, in 1689. It was rebuilt a year later only to be destroyed by the French again in 1693, this time with 27,000 pounds of gun powder. Lightning struck again in 1764—more destruction. The powers that be began to lose interest at this point, preferring to build their own palaces elsewhere in a newer, more convenient style, and the castle was gradually gutted for building materials. Victor Hugo wrote of the castle upon his visit in 1838: "What times it has been through! Five hundred years long it has been victim to everything that has shaken Europe, and now it has collapsed under its weight."

The castle had become by then, in its ruinousness, an icon of Romanticism—which points to another obstacle in forgetting at this scale: The decomposition of a castle, unlike that of a body or a house, is picturesque. Once abandoned by kings, counts, dukes, prince electors, emperors, and generals, Heidelberg Castle was taken over by artists. The question then became, in the nineteenth century: Do you preserve the castle or do you preserve the ruin? Where is the meaning, the locus of power now—in what was built and its reasons why? or in what has passed and the reasons why of its passing? Or does it lie in the aesthetic now-ness of ruins, in textures of crumbling rather than brightness?

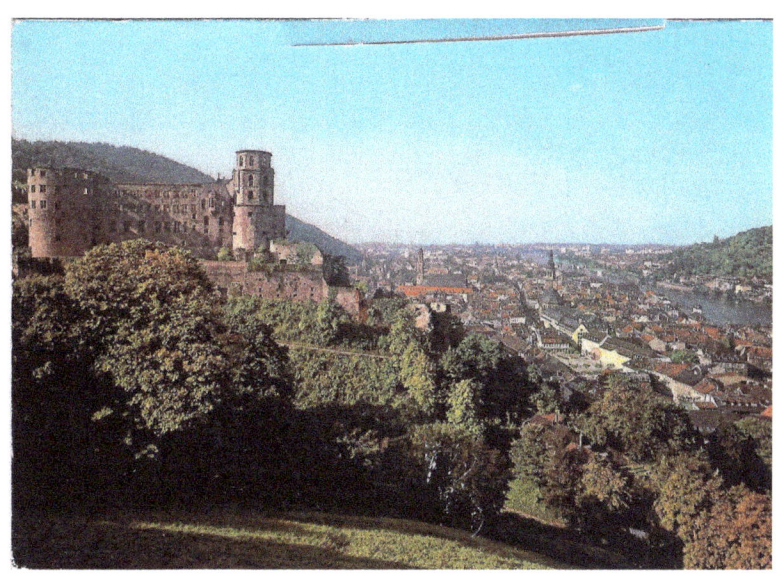

There is a castle not far from this little valley, in the mountains to the east, about an hour by car. This is true: a real castle. It's made of stone and wrought iron and glass and, like most castles in the American West, it was built by one man; his name is Jim Bishop. In 1959, at the age of 15, Bishop purchased a two and a half acre parcel on an isolated stretch of wooded highway for $450 and began, with his father, to build a family cabin. Over the course of the 1970s, however, while the hippies over here were pitching their teepees, the cabin evolved by force of a certain specifically American madness into a castle—towers, parapets, stained glass cathedral windows, the works.

It there a technical definition of a castle? Is there a book somewhere of best practices and standards to which this castle might petition entry and which it might, upon it's very likely rejection, decry as a relic of Eurocentric elitism? It's one thing to build a castle on a hill when you're taxing the life out of ten thousand peasants; it's quite another when you're just a guy with an ornamental iron works business in Pueblo. It's pretty clear from the many hand-painted signs propped up around the property what Jim Bishop thinks about taxes; he's had a leg up from no one, he's his own man—refuses even to charge admission, and opens his castle to all comers. When I was there, one October afternoon, it was packed, lines of cars parked up and down the highway. He doesn't like rules either, so there aren't any, you can climb any perilous wrought iron staircase you like, he only asks that you don't do anything stupid. It is "this belief in America being a Free Country made up of Free Persons," the castle's website declares, that "has fueled [Bishop's] passions in building the castle to represent the American Dream in an undeniably tangible and awe inspiring form!"[8]

In a "historical vacuum," the individual blazes.

Look at Heidelberg Castle and you see centuries, armies, wars and struggles, phases of destruction, layers of ownership like rings in a tree. Look at Bishop Castle and you see—what? A singular vision. A feat. The weird, awesome force of human initiative. In the words of the website: "A monumental statue in stone and iron that cries loud testament to the beauty and glory of not only Having a Dream, but Sticking with your Dream no matter what, and most importantly, that if you do believe in yourself and strive to maintain that belief, anything can happen!"

History is like tapestry. History is like compost. History is like a roadmap through time, only seen in reverse; or a thoughtmap laid over time (whatever that is) in retrospect. There are lines, there are paths, there are tangled threads, but there is also compaction and lithification. And there is also space. Five hundred years of time is vast and vacant. It is full of forgetting. Forgetting is the erosion of the matter of the world in a process sympathetic to the erosion of matter in the brain. History is a certain kind of space, then, with certain paths through, certain threads, with certain compaction simultaneously.

Great men forge the paths—this is one theory. Martin Luther changed the whole world by forging the path of the man accountable only to God. The enormity of this particular turn, this first step, is staggering, awe inspiring. It's true that he did this—he stood up by his conscience to the throne of power—and that he possessed the will, the personality, the pathology, perhaps, to weather the fallout.

It may also be true that the paths present themselves to be forged, and that, in each case, some first man or other is bound to stumble down them; that it is the path, in fact, that makes greatness of him, at least so far and so long as it needs him. In this sense, the path of individualism made Luther; in little more than an instant it then barreled over him and he spent much of his later life struggling unsuccessfully to contain what he'd unleashed. So what then, exactly, is the path? A thousand small evolutions leading into a current. An endless interplay of compounding (memory) and vaporization (forgetting).

There is a path between Luther and Jim Bishop's castle. There is a path between Luther and Joseph Goebbels. There is a path between Luther's disputation in Heidelberg, which lurks invisibly, unmarked, in this packet of postcards, and my path up the road through the aspens to the gate.

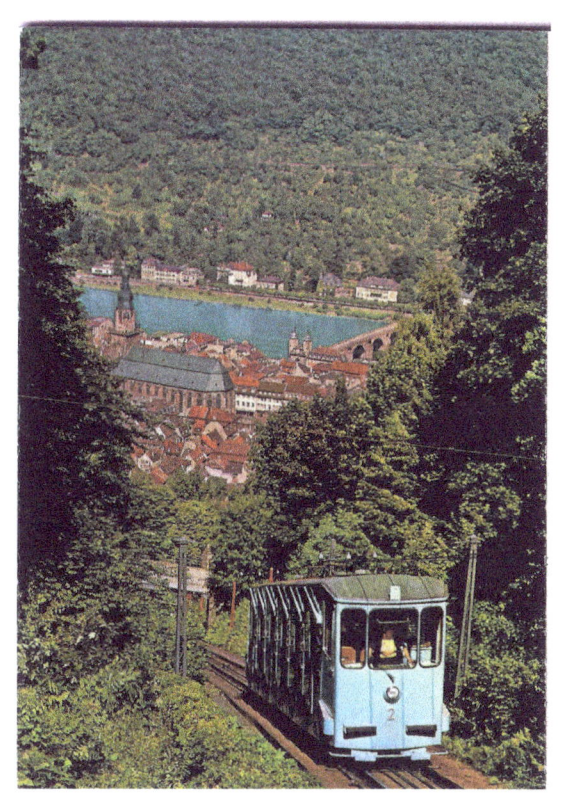

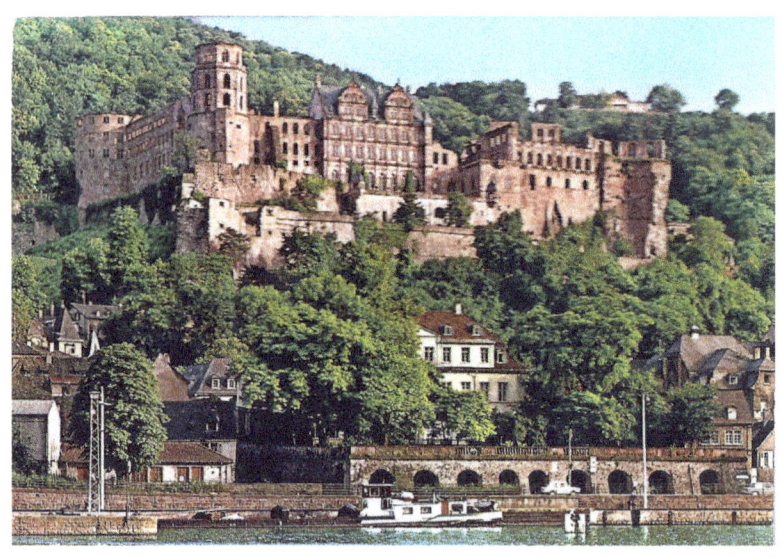

Forgetting is evaporation behind; blindness is forgetting forward.

There are nineteen cards in the packet because one has been, for some reason, removed. The long accordion is in two pieces, with frayed edges on ends where the missing picture had been. Someone took it, I presume, for some purpose or another, perhaps the person who dropped the rest in the trash. Later, however, I found the missing picture, by itself, in the desk. It depicts a narrow, charming street lined with shops, filled with then-young, now-old people on vacation. It's an orphan of an orphan now, that one stray picture.

I am uneasy, still, about taking the packet. It took taking the packet once and for all to find that it really isn't mine. It sits there now on the shelf beside my desk but it sits inert, not blooming or growing into my room like some of the various objects around it—the Indonesian figurine that was a gift from my mother for luck and prosperity that I've broken three times and glued back together; the bookcase that is my favorite bookcase, that belonged to my husband before we were together; the marble swan bookends that were also a gift, one of which is now headless and missing a wing; the framed map of the Dakotas from 1903 that I found online surprisingly cheap and that feels thus like a gift from the archives of history. I take pleasure in gifts; gifts are the home's aristocratic objects. I don't take pleasure, it turns out, in things that I've taken without permission.

I will return the packet next time I go to the house. I can say from this, certainly: It is wrong to steal. It is also true and perhaps more accurate to say that I simply got what I wanted. I scanned all the pictures; I learned something about what I wanted in taking them; I made something out of them that is now mine and will soon be nobody's—it's enough. Art colonizes. None of this is mine to take: the postcards, the house, the valley, the life, the city (Heidelberg), its long history. But then, what is really mine? This air I breathe? This land I stand on? These people I love? This body I dwell in? All these thoughts, which will one day just go out? Art partakes, just as life partakes.

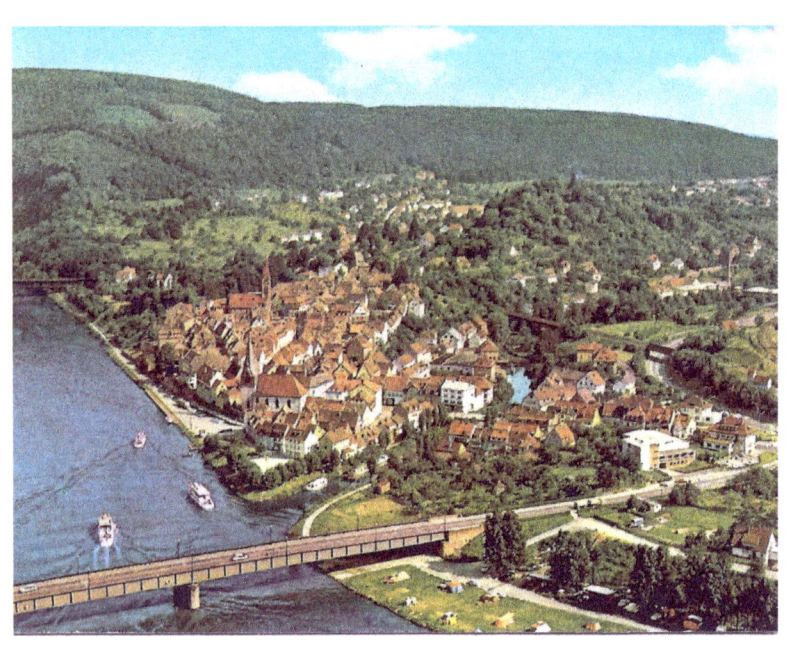

The man whose house this once was built the house in a state not of embarking but returning, or perhaps a state of embarking upon his return. There are large parts of his life I know nothing about. He went to New York, I believe; he had relationships, surely; he was involved in the theater. But he returned, eventually, to Colorado. The comfort of the house, I believe, stems largely from this: By the time he built it, he knew what he was about. The house has a stable feeling; it's happy where it's at, and is no longer searching.

The last time I was there I came across an album of photographs from the 1980s. Most of the photographs depicted gatherings of one sort or another in the house: big dinners around the long table; children sprawled on the living room floor; family and friends in easy clusters, on the chairs, on the floor, on the step leading up to the kitchen; conversations; laughter; adults with wine glasses, cigarettes, or guitars. The room itself is just the same. The people, though, are like sparks, like smoke, like ghosts, like a translucent overlay on the room that I know, that is minutely and very minorly—at least at this moment, while I am alone here, looking at the pictures—mine. The vibe in the pictures is comfortable, welcoming, happy, settled. The sheen of those bright, idealistic bodies is gone; they have weight, now, in the pictures, perhaps because they have jobs and children; they have cares of a prosaic rather than a utopian sort. They are surprised, perhaps, to find themselves in the eighties, as I am to find myself in the third decade, already, of the twenty-first century. But a dinner party is the greatest form of now, and in the context of the pictures, at least, they've forgotten time in favor of each other.

A man's house is his castle, here in America. This man found his, it seems, in this quiet valley. There are no tourists parking cars up and down the side of the highway, only friends. It's nice. Their talk warms the house and lives in its walls.

It is of "the great silence of the historical vacuum," whether real imagined, or partially real, or complicatedly imagined, that I am myself, above all, a product. The man whose house this once was knew what he was leaving in Denmark. I have never left anything and never arrived anywhere, nor do I have anything behind or below me, save the domestic objects of personal memory. I own what I love. But I feel myself to be aerosol in nature, not layered and compacted. The part of me that knew what he was leaving in Denmark is four generations removed from my consciousness; the knowledge is inaccessible to me, except perhaps as a certain strain of independence and the very faintest streak of longing.

I look at Heidelberg and I think of breathing. I think: The air over there must be very thick; thick with moisture and oxygen from all those trees, and thick also with the atmosphere of history. Here in this valley, I know how to breathe, in this dry, thin air, at 8,000 feet above sea level, where very little was ever built. What is it like to breathe there, at 375 feet, with 800-year-old monasteries hanging in the air? And ancient Roman encampments and synagogues in flames?

It is to breathe that one travels, most elementally. To breathe the air of a different place. A souvenir has nothing to do with that; it is a marker, merely, independent of the senses. More specifically, perhaps, it's a catalytic device, whether in regard to memory (in the case of the purchaser) or imagination (in the case of the recipient). I would like, one day, to go to Heidelberg. Maybe I will. But my love of this object, the packet of postcards, has nothing to do with the prospect of travel; it has to do with all that the object itself contains right here, in this moment, in the place where it is.

As I write all this, no travel is possible—due to breathing, in fact; specifically, a virus transmitted via aerosol particles that encircled the globe in a matter of weeks, from one exhale to another inhale, breath to breath, across every continent, over oceans in airplanes, across countries in cars, in buses, in trains, into cities and towns, into restaurants and bars and schools and hospitals, into living rooms, into bedrooms, everywhere. Our trips were all canceled; our airline tickets were transformed into credits and languish there now in abstraction while we sit at home. But swift and agile as a virus (for better or worse) is this mind, which reads and walks and considers and imagines.

Endnotes

[1] Cécile Poulot, "Hot Potato Heritage: Heidelberg's Nazi Amphitheatre," *Failed Architecture*, October 4, 2017.
[2] Wikipedia, "Heidelberg," https://en.wikipedia.org/wiki/Heidelberg.
[3] Quoted in Rev. Christopher Maronde, "The Heidelberg Disputation," LutheranReformation.org, October 17, 2017.
[4] Steven E. Aschheim, "Hannah Arendt and Karl Jaspers: Friendship, Catastrophe and the Possibilities of German-Jewish Dialogue," *Culture and Catastrophe*, Palgrave Macmillan, 1996.
[5] William James, "On Some Mental Effects of the Earthquake," *William James: Writings 1902-1910*, The Library of America, 1987.
[6] Jaspers, Karl, "The Question of German Guilt," transl. E. B. Ashton, Fordham University Press, 2000.
[7] Hannah Arendt, *The Origins of Totalitarianism*, Harcourt Inc., 1994. (Originally published 1951.)
[8] Bishop's Castle, https://www.bishopcastle.org/about/.

www.ingramcontent.com/pod-product-compliance
Lightning Source LLC
Chambersburg PA
CBHW040521220526
45473CB00013B/2938